PS1 focus groups

CULTURAL PROCESSES IN CHILD DEVELOPMENT

The Minnesota Symposia on Child Psychology

Volume 29

CULTURAL PROCESSES IN CHILD DEVELOPMENT

The Minnesota Symposia on Child Psychology

Volume 29

Edited by

Ann S. Masten
University of Minnesota

LAWRENCE ERLBAUM ASSOCIATES, PUBLISHERS
1999   Mahwah, New Jersey   London

Lawrence Erlbaum Associates, Inc., Publishers
10 Industrial Avenue
Mahwah, New Jersey 07430

Cover design by Kathryn Houghtaling Lacey

Library of Congress Cataloging-in-Publication Data

Cultural processes in child development / edited by Ann S. Masten.
          p.   cm. -- (The Minnesota symposia on child psychology ; v.
29)
    Papers from the 29th Minnesota Symposium on Child Psychology, held
in October 1994 at the University of Minnesota.
    Includes bibliographical references and index,
    ISBN 0-8058-2167-8 (alk. paper)
    1. Child development--Cross-cultural studies--Congresses.
2. Child psychology--Cross-cultural studies--Congresses.
I. Masten, Ann S. II. Minnesota Symposium on Child Psychology (29th
: 1994 : University of Minnesota) III. Series: Minnesota symposia
on child psychology (Series) ; v. 29.
HQ767.9.C83 1998
305.231--dc21   98-47096
                                                         CIP

Books published by Lawrence Erlbaum Associates are printed on acid-free paper,
and their bindings are chosen for strength and durability.

Printed in the United States of America
10   9   8   7   6   5   4   3   2   1

Contributors

Linda M. Burton

Department of Human Development and Family Studies
S-110 Henderson Building
The Pennsylvania State University
University Park, PA 16802

Catherine R. Cooper

Department of Psychology
University of California, Santa Cruz
221 Clark Kerr Hall
Santa Cruz, CA 95064

Shirley Brice Heath

Department of English
Stanford University
Stanford, CA 94305

Katherine Magnuson

Education Department
Brown University
Providence, RI 02912

Eric H. Durbrow

Department of Human Development and Family Studies
S-110 Henderson Building
The Pennsylvania State University
University Park, PA 16802

Vonnie C. McLoyd

Center for Human Growth and Development
University of Michigan
300 North Ingalls
Ann Arbor, MI 48109

Cynthia García Coll

Education Department
Brown University
Providence, RI 02912

Townsand Price-Spratlen

Department of Sociology
300 Bricker Hall
Ohio State University
190 North Oval Mall
Columbus, OH 43210

Richard A. Shweder

Committee on Human Development
University of Chicago
5730 South Woodlawn Avenue
Chicago, IL 60637

Contents

Preface

The chapters of this volume were originally presented at the 29th Minnesota Symposium on Child Psychology, held in October 1994 at the University of Minnesota, Minneapolis. The focus of this symposium on cultural processes in child development emerged from the growing recognition among us at the Institute of Child Development and many others in the field that we need to know more about the processes linking individual development and the contexts in which it occurs, and that this is no longer a luxury but essential for good science and good policy in an increasingly interconnected and pluralistic world.

The importance of cultural processes has been acknowledged in child development texts for many years, but typically relegated to the chapter on theory, for example in discussions of Bronfenbrenner's (1979) classic ecocultural model, or the chapter on "culture" in the section on contexts of development. The segregation of culture to special sections echoed the status of cultural processes in the scientific disciplines concerned with child development. Now serious movement toward integration is apparent in a revival of interest in culture and child development (Harkness & Super, 1996; Jessor, Colby, & Shweder, 1996; Shweder et al., 1998; Tronick, 1992). The chapters in this volume reflect not only the surge of interest in cultural processes in developmental science, but also a search for deeper understanding of how culture "gets into" the individual child, shaping and being shaped by development.

The authors of this volume chronicle the challenges as well as the benefits of venturing out to the growing edge of theory and research concerned with how cultures and individuals interact to shape development. These investigators have wrestled with the complexities of figuring out the assumptions, beliefs, values, and rules by which peoples conceptualize their lives and rear their children, organize their societies, and educate the next generation. For example, they seek to understand whether it makes a difference where children sleep, whether a child holds minority status in a society, how to know when you are mistaking the universal for the particular or the particular for the universal in child development. They have struggled with the paradox of the insider's perspective, where an insider view may be essential to a valid description of socialization and development in a given society although insiders could be blind to the central qualities of their culture because they take them for granted. They recognize that an individual, including an investigator, may become aware of his or her own cultural beliefs and assumptions only when faced with a dramatically different set of assumptions. Most provocatively, perhaps, they have thought about whether it even makes sense to distinguish "person" and "context."

In the first chapter, García Coll and Magnuson emphasize the necessity for a revolutionary shift in the way we do business if culture is to be integrated meaningfully into developmental research. They argue that the questions we ask, the measures we use, our conceptualizations of development, our data analysis and interpretations will all need to shift in order to realize the potential of assimilating culture into our enterprise. For some, even the conceptualization of what constitutes science will need to change, if culture is to be studied in relation to development, rather than ignored or tolerated as noise in a laboratory experiment. These authors draw on their studies of young mothers in the United States and Puerto Rico to illustrate their points.

The multifaceted shift they describe represents a guide to "unpacking" culture, a theme Cooper develops in her chapter as well. In chapter 2, Cooper describes three studies that illustrate how she and her colleagues have integrated three models in their efforts to bring developmental and cultural perspectives together. Their studies have engaged adolescents from multiple cultures observed in the varied contexts of their everyday lives, incorporating concepts from the ecocultural model (that considers multiple dimensions of culture, ranging from activity settings to values), the multiple worlds approach (that addresses processes by which adolescents bridge the multiple contexts they must negotiate as they move among from family, school, and peers contexts), and parallel designs, where analyses include within- and across-cultural comparisons. In addition, Cooper's work, like that of García Coll and Magnuson, illustrates how the rich information gleaned from focus groups can flesh out the bones of variable-focused data analysis, bringing process to life.

In the third chapter, Heath's account of language development among adolescents in youth organizations provides a detailed look at how one of the multiple worlds of adolescence could influence development and how language can serve as a mediator of ongoing socialization and enculturation. In this chapter, Heath draws on more than a decade of work on language in voluntary youth organizations to illustrate the role of language in socialization and vice versa. Through ethnographic observation and analysis of discourse in these organizations, Heath and her colleagues have delineated processes that shape language and, in turn, learning and socialization. The work Heath describes is also important in moving the study of language development beyond the early years of life.

The chapter by Burton and Price-Spratlen also illustrates the complexities of understanding any one of a child's multiple worlds, in this case the "neighborhood." They address the methodological issues they and others must confront in order to capture meaningful processes connecting this world to child development. Their points are illustrated by descriptions of their multigenerational study of African American families in 18 neighborhoods. For example, they point out the challenges of defining neighborhood when the perspectives of child, parent, and investigator may differ markedly. A child may think of neighborhood in terms of where he or she spends time, whereas an investigator may be measuring features of a census tract that have little correspondence to the child-defined world. Among some cultural groups, as is the case among families they studied, children reside with kith and kin in several homes and physical neighborhoods that cut across geographical boundaries. They also describe how neighborhoods, however defined, may differ in character by time of day (i.e., having diurnal rhythms), change over longer periods of time, and developmentally transform. Moreover, although most models assume neighborhood-to-child influences, it is quite conceivable that children and adolescents have an active role in shaping neighborhoods both through their choices of defining the neighborhood and in the ways their behaviors affect the nature of their neighborhoods. Burton and Price-Spratlen remind us that culture and context themselves have the dynamic features of other living systems, with transactional influences among their constituent subsystems and the macrosystems in which they are embedded, daily and seasonal variations, and developmental transformation.

Durbrow's chapter moves us to the study of culture and development outside the United States where, as a developmental anthropologist, he has confronted many of the same conceptual and methodological issues faced by investigators of diverse cultures within U.S. society. He draws on data from his field studies of Caribbean cultures to illustrate how anthropology and psychology, with their relative emphasis on emic and etic perspectives, respectively, can be integrated in the study of development. Durbrow and colleagues have developed a method of ascertaining the criteria by which adults in a culture evaluate the progress of socialization in their children. The fact that adults evaluate how children are doing, based on their values and goals, appears to be universal, though the nature of those standards and values may differ dramatically in content.

Durbrow makes an evolutionary argument for why such criteria would be adaptive and then discusses the competence criteria of villages he has studied using both the ethnographic and observational tools of the anthropologist and the psychometric tools of a child psychologist.

In the last two chapters, the discussants at this Symposium reflect on the methodological and conceptual issues attendant on the current movement to bring culture and development together in science. Vonnie McLoyd elucidates the challenges faced by investigators who want to capture relevant dimensions of the complex, overlapping, and embedded cultural contexts of U.S. society. She discusses cultural validity as a central goal in this endeavor and the need for advances in theory and methodology to facilitate progress, drawing on examples from the work presented in this volume. In closing, McLoyd calls for a comprehensive and proactive effort by educators, professional societies, granting agencies, and scientific journal editors to provide the training and resources necessary for bringing culture into developmental science.

In the concluding chapter, Richard Shweder places this Symposium in historical context by contrasting structural views of mental development with the perspectives of contemporary cultural psychology. On the one hand, he questions developmental principles purporting to be universal, such as those embodied by Piaget's stage theory of mental development, that result in most non-Western adults being classified as "immature" thinkers. On the other hand, cultural pluralists tend to throw the baby out with the bath water in rejecting all structural ideas about cognitive development. He points to the potential for transformation when psychologists recognize the variety in how mature, capable humans think and anthropologists recognize the role of basic processes of rationality in human cognition in constructing our diverse senses of reality. In other words, Shweder reminds us that it is possible to be cognitively mature in culturally diverse ways as a result of the same fundamental processes in development.

As a whole, this volume reflects the beginnings of a "cultural renaissance" in developmental science. At the Symposium itself, we explored many additional topics in small-group discussions, including transcultural adoption, the effects of war on development, the role of culture in the development of self-concepts, and the challenge of defining child mental health across culture. Many other topics were explored in conversations between sessions. We left with a deeper awareness of both the challenges of understanding cultural processes in development and the necessity of proceeding.

The Symposium is a treasured tradition of the institute of Child Development which could not happen without the energy, enthusiasm, and efforts of the students, staff, and faculty of the "Tute." On their behalf, I want to express our deep appreciation to the speakers who authored papers and came to Minnesota to deliver them and to the discussion leaders who moderated the often lively debates on special topics, including Patricia Bauer, Harold Grotevant, George Realmuto, Richard Weinberg, and Carolyn Williams. Lujean Huffman-Nordberg, Claudia Johnston, Art Sesma, and Shane Jimerson provided wonderful technical support of many kinds for the Symposium. Special thanks are due as well to the team of students who served on the Institute's "cultural diversity team," which came up with the topic for this symposium as one of their efforts to infuse our teaching and scholarship with a deeper appreciation and knowledge of cultural issues and processes in development. They included Poldi Gerard-Ngo, Jordan Hart, Lisa Rohleder, Arturo Sesma, Recket Si-Asar, and Adrian Teo. Financial support through the University of Minnesota for this Symposium was provided by the Institute of Child Development (Richard Weinberg, Director), the College of Education and Human Development (Robert Bruininks, Dean), the Biobehavioral Training Grant in Developmental Disabilities (Megan Gunnar, Robert Blum, and Charles A. Nelson, Directors) funded by the National Institute of Child Health and Human Development, and a grant to Ann Masten from the Bush Faculty Development Program on Excellence and Diversity in Teaching.

REFERENCES

Bronfenbrenner, U. (1979). *The ecology of human development.* Cambridge, MA: Harvard University Press.

Harkness, S., & Super, C. M. (1996). *Parents' cultural belief systems: Their origins, expression, and consequences.* New York: Guilford Press.

Jessor, R., Colby, A., & Shweder, R. A. (1996). *Ethnography and human development: Context and meaning in social inquiry.* Chicago: University of Chicago Press.

Shweder, R. A., Goodnow, J., Hatano, G., Levine, R., Markus, H., & Miller, P. (1998). The cultural psychology of development: One mind, many mentalities. In W. Damon (Editor-in-Chief), R. M. Lerner (Vol. Ed.), *Handbook of child psychology. Vol. 1: Theoretical models of human development* (5th ed., pp. 865-937). New York: Wiley.

Tronick, E. Z. (Ed., Special Section). (1992). Introduction: Cross-cultural studies of development. *Developmental Psychology, 28,* 566-567.

Chapter 1

Cultural Influences on Child Development: Are We Ready for a Paradigm Shift?

Cynthia García Coll
Katherine Magnuson
Brown University

There is a vast tradition of cross-cultural as well as intracultural research that examines the influence of cultural processes on child development. The work by John and Beatrice Whiting, Robert Levine, Michael Cole, Sarah Harkness, Charles Super, Barbara Rogoff, among others, contribute to our knowledge base in this area (see Cole & Bruner, 1974; Levine, 1973; Rogoff & Morelli, 1989; Super & Harkness, 1980; Triandis & Heron, 1981; Whiting & Whiting, 1975). However, this research tends to remain at the periphery of our knowledge base about developmental processes during childhood (Slaughter-Defoe, Nakagawa, Takanishi, & Johnson, 1990). Our discipline's high regard for carefully controlled experimental studies and the use of standardized psychometrically sound assessments makes us hesitant to use qualitative or nonexperimental methodologies and prone to disregard the findings obtained with such methods (Hoshmand & Polkinghorne, 1992; Kessen, 1993; Levine, 1980). This continues today despite the fact that we are beginning to realize that these alternative methodologies might be more appropriate in capturing the complexity of the interplay between cultural and developmental processes.

The main argument presented in this chapter is that in order for us to be able to fully comprehend the impact of cultural processes on child development, we have to be open to the use of multiple methods of inquiry, assessment, analysis, and interpretation. If we are serious about the importance of studying cultural influences on child development, a new approach and openness to diverse research methodologies is necessary. The basic question then becomes: Are we ready for a paradigm shift?

1

A paradigm shift will be necessary (see Harkness, 1980) in order to place cultural processes at the *core* and not at the periphery of our conceptualizations and investigations of developmental processes. If we are serious about studying cultural processes influence on children's development, then theory and research on these topics must consistently be placed at the originating point of our scientific endeavors.

Our discipline has traditionally started with the individual organism—the child—and conceptualized it as the product of intrinsic biological processes (including maturation), of the *immediate* environment, and more recently of a combination of the two (Sameroff & Chandler, 1975). The proposed paradigm shift will also start with the individual child, but will conceptualize most of the environmental influences on the child as a primary reflection of cultural processes and as a major medium for developmental change. Cultural context has to be conceptualized as more than the background against which development unfolds and instead, as a major source of influence on these processes (Cole, 1992). Moreover, cultural context will be as much a part of the analyses of developmental processes of children in other cultures as *for our own* culture.

We have to recognize that the cultural pressures of our own society, like any other society, modify and define the developmental processes of our children. Consequently, our research on developmental processes should consider the influences of our own cultural and sociohistorical locations (Elder, Modell, & Parke, 1993; Newson & Newson, 1974). We can be described as a 20th-century society that is very ethnically and racially diverse, industrialized, includes urban, rural, small, and large communities, is subject to rapid changes (including fundamental changes in family structure), and emphasizes autonomy, individuality, cognitive development, and segregation (by age, socioeconomic class, and race; Holtzman, Díaz-Guerrero, & Swartz, 1975; Kessen, 1993; Newson & Newson, 1974; Super & Harkness, 1994). These characteristics need to be taken as locations for studying developmental processes in our developmental laboratories.

This chapter concentrates on the methodological implications of this paradigm shift. The main argument is that in most areas of inquiry about cultural and developmental processes, the standard scientific ways of conducting developmental research need to be examined carefully and even questioned as to their validity and applicability. Specifically, placing cultural processes at the core of developmental research has profound implications for the kind of questions we ask, the research designs that we use, the instruments or assessment tools that we employ, the way we analyze the data and the interpretations of our findings. Essentially, all aspects of the scientific process are affected . . . therefore, it constitutes a paradigm shift. The rest of this chapter illustrates, with examples from our own research and that of others, the methodological implications of this paradigm shift.

THE KINDS OF QUESTIONS WE ASK

> To handle the complexities of person in context, researchers should study process with outcome using appropriately complex methods such as the dynamic assessment of interaction as it unfolds over time, assessment in multiple contexts, including variations in tasks and contextual supports and participatory observation. (Wozniak & Fisher, 1993, xii)

A central part of any paradigm is the questions that researchers seek to answer. A major part of proposing a paradigm shift is suggesting that we begin to ask *new* questions in our research or *old* questions in different ways. When culture is no longer seen as a passive background upon which development unfolds, but rather as an active part of the changes and influences on developmental processes, the questions that researchers pose become much more complex. The complexity arises, in part, from the need to operationalize not only the multiple facets of culture, but also the interactions among these multiple facets. As Szaponick and Kurtines (1993) asserted, "if we are interested in studying cultural context, we have to study it as it really occurs, rather than some idealized concept of indigenous culture" (p. 400). This new treatment of culture reflects the need to "unpackage" culture, that is to consider culture as a multidimensional evolving source of influence on developmental processes within any culture rather than as a monolithic nominal variable (Cooper, 1994; Weisner, Gallimore, & Jordan, 1988; B. Whiting, 1976). The unpacking of culture also requires researchers to operationalize culture in concrete variables (Segall, 1986).

How does changing the questions that we ask affect the rest of the research process? Let's take for example the question "What determines how mothers interact with their infants in different cultural systems?" Tables 1.1 and 1.2 show analyses of mother–infant interaction data in 37

TABLE 1.1
Correlations Between Maternal Age, Number of Adults,
Caretaking Experience, and Maternal Behaviors During Feeding

Maternal Behaviors	Maternal Age	No. of Adults	Caretaking Experience
Visual Contact	−.23	−.01	−.21
Vocal Behaviors			
Praises	.29	.36*	.42*
Comments	.01	.08	.20
Physical Contact			
Instrumental	.26	−.11	−.09
Affectionate	.21	.43**	.11
Expressive Behaviors			
Smiling	−.09	.23	−.18

*$p < .05$.
**$p < .01$.

TABLE 1.2
Correlations Between Maternal Age, Number of Adults, Previous
Caretaking Experience, and Ainsworth's Ratings During Feeding

	Maternal Age	No. of Adults	Caretaking Experience
Determination of Feedings	.36*	.18	.36*
Amount of Interaction	.52**	.50**	.39*
Appropriateness of Initiations	.42**	.37*	.03
Quality of Physical Contact	.12	.38*	.04

$*p < .05.$
$**p < .01.$

primiparous, low SES, mothers ranging from 14 to 27 years of age in San Juan, Puerto Rico. We have argued elsewhere that the cultural context of teenage childbearing within a traditional low socioeconomic status Puerto Rican culture is relatively supportive and conducive to optimal parenting and developmental outcomes in their children—more so than in contexts where early parenting is not as normative (see García Coll, 1989; García Coll, Escobar, Cebollero, & Valcárcel, 1989; García Coll & Vázquez García, 1995). Table 1.1 shows the data for the discrete behaviors shown by the mothers during the first feeding interactions with their newborns, derived from videotapes which were coded later by an observer unaware of the mother's characteristics. Table 1.2 shows qualitative rating scales filled out by the same observers at the end of the coding session which capture more subjective aspects of the interaction.

The first thing to be noted is the kind of variables that are included in the analyses. Patterns of mother–infant interaction are not viewed exclusively as the product of individual maternal characteristics. Other variables that are conceptualized as the product of the interactions between the cultural context and the individual, are considered in the analyses. For example, the mothers' report of the number of adults that will be helping her with child care and her previous experience in child care are measured. These two variables can be conceptualized as a function of the extent to which the culture supports mothers regardless of their age in their maternal role and how it permits children to take care of other children, as well as the interests and competencies of the particular individual.

Our results suggest that the pattern of associations between these variables and mother–infant interaction was different depending on the aspects of the interaction that were measured. Specifically, there were stronger associations between contextual variables and qualitative aspects of the interaction than discrete behaviors. It is interesting to note also that maternal age (an individual characteristic) was more strongly associated with qualitative aspects of the interaction than the actual behaviors per se. Thus both contextual and individual variables were more strongly associated with *how* mothers behaved than with what they actually did.

To provide additional illustration of the complexity of the questions, let us examine the findings from another study which investigated the determinants of mother–infant interaction patterns in adolescent mothers, within a lower to middle-class Caucasian population in Providence, Rhode Island (see Levine, García Coll, & Oh, 1985 for more detailed description of the study). Following the same conceptual framework, whereby patterns of mother–infant interaction are conceived as determined by both individual characteristics (maternal age, education, and ego development) and culturally defined contextual variables (child-care support), interactional patterns were observed as a function of these variables in two different contexts: in a face-to-face and a teaching situation. In general, different patterns of predictor variables were significantly related to both mother and infant behavior in each of the situations, as Table 1.3 shows. During face-to-face interaction, ego development was the best predictor of positive affect (as measured by mutual gaze and contingency), followed by child-

TABLE 1.3
Effects of Ego Development, Total Child-Care Support,
Education, and Maternal Age on Mother–Infant Interaction

Dependent Variable	*Independent Variable*	*F*	*P*	*Multiple R*
Maternal behaviors during face-to-face interaction				
Positive Affect	Ego development, child-care support	4.26	< .05	.52
Mutual Gaze	Ego development, child-care support	4.25	< .05	.52
% Contingency to infant behavior	Ego development, maternal age, child-care support	6.11	< .01	.73
Maternal behaviors during teaching tasks				
Demonstrates tasks	Maternal age	4.83	< .05	.42
Takes away object	Child-care support, education, maternal age	3.73	< .05	.59
Verbalizations	Maternal age	4.79	< .05	.42
Positive affect	Child-care support	4.35	< .05	.40
Infant behaviors during face-to-face interaction				
Vocalizations	Education, child-care support	4.11	< .05	.51
Smiling	Ego development, child-care support, maternal age	3.47	< .05	.57

*p < .05.
**p < .01.
Note. From Levine, García Coll, and Oh (1985). Reproduced with permission.

care support. Thus, both individual and contextually driven variables accounted for significant percentages of the variance in maternal behavior during face-to-face interactions with the infants. A less systematic pattern of association was found for behaviors during the teaching context. Child-care support was the best predictor in removal of objects and positive affect, whereas maternal age was the best predictor in demonstrations of tasks and verbalizations. Thus in two different situations the best predictors included both individually and contextually driven variables; however the predictive power of these variables significantly changed across different contexts. By looking at the influence of multiple variables across various contexts and aspects of mother–infant interaction, the question has changed from "what are the determinants of mother–infant interaction across all contexts?" to "*under which circumstances are some variables more powerful predictors than others?*" . . . or to "*which aspects of maternal and infant behavior can contextual and individual characteristics predict?*"

RESEARCH DESIGN

In the past decade we have shifted our strategy: instead of focusing on cross-cultural variations in products of development [developmental outcome] . . . [we] began to seek an understanding of the role of culture in the process of developmental change. . . . The shift from the study of products to processes has led to a substantial change in research strategy . . . instead of engaging in cross-cultural research in which culture is treated as an independent variable in the classic sense, we have sought to understand the general mechanisms by means of which culture as a medium constitutes both human learning and development. This has led us to focus on children in our own society and on the creation of special learning environments within which to study the process of change. (Cole, 1992, p. 283)

As this quote exemplifies, the necessary change from studying developmental outcomes to developmental processes specified within a cultural context results in a major shift in research design. This constitutes a major aspect of the proposed paradigm shift, and is essentially a shift from a cross-cultural comparative research design to a within-culture analysis.

In the past, most studies designed to study cultural influences on child development have used comparative methods whereby cross-cultural comparisons are conducted of developmental outcomes at a single point in time (Holtzman, Díaz-Guerrero, & Swartz, 1975). This approach has for the most part not paid particular attention to the processes that lead to the differences in developmental outcome. For example, Graham (1992) after reviewing the literature in the field's major journals on Black children reported that most studies were comparative in design. These studies, which for the most part have charted the losses of Black children relative to White children, have failed to provide us with a better understanding of these children's repertoire of adaptive social behaviors or intellectual potentials. Similarly, Slaughter-Defoe et al.'s review of research (1990) on Asian American's school success found that the cultural attributions made in these studies were almost solely defined in reference to values, attitudes, and beliefs rather than socioeconomic status, family structures, or neighborhood and community factors. By not empirically addressing the mechanisms by which these differences in outcome arise, research has disregarded within group variability and has in many cases confounded cultural differences with differences in socioeconomic status or other variables that might explain the differences observed in outcome (Betancourt & López, 1993; García Coll et al., 1996, Goduka, Poole, & Aotaki-Phenice, 1992; Graham, 1992; Harkness, 1980).

A good example of a study illustrating the importance of examining processes and within group variability was conducted by Chen and Stevenson (1989). The researchers looked at school achievement and homework across three cultures: The United States, China, and Japan. The findings showed a discrepancy between associating homework and achievement across cultures and within cultures. Across cultures the amount of time spent on homework and parental assistance was positively related to achievement. Within cultures there was no significant relation between the amount of time a child spent on homework or parental assistance and achievement. Chen and Stevenson suggested that within a particular culture the child who spent the most time on his homework was not necessarily the better student, and conversely that spending too little time on homework might indicate that the child was not benefiting enough from the exercises. Thus, they concluded that to understand the association between homework and achievement across cultures, variables such as parental assistance and time spent on homework were predictive, but to understand associations within cultures that it might be more revealing to look at the content and enjoyment level of the homework assignments.

Another study of family characteristics and developmental outcomes that illustrates why it is necessary to consider the mechanisms and processes by which variables influence outcomes across a variety of contexts was conducted by Goduka et al. (1992). The researchers studied family characteristics and developmental outcomes of Black children in three rural South African contexts: the homeland, the resettlement, and white-owned farms. Although all three areas suffered economic hardship, families in the homeland were able to provide more in terms of material resources and residential stability and these variables were associated with more positive outcomes. However, the differences between the homeland, resettlement, and the farm could not be fully captured by the family variables. As the authors explained,

In conclusion, our data illustrates why research that compares samples based on social factors is inherently limited: relations among variables and the pathways by which these variables effect development may vary across contexts. Thus, social address models fail to consider the mechanisms by which particular family characteristics affect children. . . . Once researchers have related a descriptive variable to developmental outcomes it would be more theoretically productive to make alternate predictions about why that variable is sometimes associated with specific domains, and to test those predictions across a variety of environments. . . . It is likely that relations between these alternatives will be fairly homogeneous within a given socio-economic or residential group, making it difficult to isolate mechanisms that link family characteristics to child outcomes. However, by increasing the economic, residential, and ethnic diversity of research samples researchers would increase the chances of observing families which pair these characteristics in a variety of ways. (Goduka et al., 1992, p. 523)

In our own research on the effects of teenage childbearing on the child's developmental outcome, we have always chosen to study each group separately and operationalize the important variables within each cultural group (see García Coll & Vázquez García, 1995, for a recent summary of the studies conducted with Puerto Rican mothers). We have studied two populations simultaneously, but independently: Caucasian, mothers in Providence, Rhode Island, and Puerto Rican mothers in San Juan, Puerto Rico. In these studies, we have studied these women's experiences as mothers within a sociocultural context, and investigated various individual (psychological and demographic maternal characteristics) and contextual variables and processes which impact their adaptation to motherhood.

For example, in order to look at maternal psychological well-being after childbirth among young and old adolescent mothers and adult Puerto Rican mothers, we examined the correlations between both demographic and contextual variables that surrounded their birthing experience (see García Coll et al., 1989, for details of the study). In general, regardless of age, the mothers in San Juan reported few depressive symptoms and high maternal self-esteem. However, the analyses showed that circumstances around the marriage and pregnancy differentially affected the psychological well-being of the mothers. For instance, younger adolescents' higher depressive symptomology was associated with marriage after pregnancy. Older adolescents' higher depressive symptomology was associated with an unplanned pregnancy, but adult mothers did not present any significant correlations between depressive symptoms and any of these variables. Likewise, the study also found that stress and social support differentially affected adolescent and adult mothers. For younger adolescents, more depressive symptoms were associated with higher perceived stress, especially the number of stressful events and the perceived stress associated with these events. For older adolescents the higher depressive symptomology was correlated with a higher number of conflicts with relatives. No correlations were found between stress and support and depressive symptomology in adult mothers.

In contrast, a comparative approach was used when the question was about cultural differences in the conceptualization of adolescent child-bearing (see García Coll, 1989, for more details about the study) in these two cultures. A questionnaire was administered to mothers in Providence and San Juan to assess beliefs about teenage pregnancy and its consequences for mother and child. Our studies showed that these beliefs varied across the cultures. Specifically, marriage and childbirth were seen and accepted more often as a part of normal adolescent growth and development for Puerto Ricans. On the questionnaire, the Puerto Rican mothers reported more often than the Providence mothers that the best age for a woman to have her child is earlier in her life, that the teenage mother will naturally become a good responsible mother on her own, and that a child of a teenage mother will not have any problems if the mother and child live with her family and/or husband. A comparative approach was necessary to determine that the social context in which the Puerto Rican adolescents were located differed from the one in which Providence mothers were located. Thus, depending on the question a cross-cultural comparative analysis versus a within cultural analysis might be appropriate (Azibo, 1988).

INSTRUMENTS AND ASSESSMENT TOOLS

IQ tests are constructed to measure specific aspects of intelligence vital for solving specific problems associated with industrialization, bureaucracy, urbanism, and the like. One should bear in mind that the cognitive skills tapped by these tests are those that Western cultures emphasize in their formal schooling. . . . Hence the primary purpose of IQ tests is to predict how well children in Western cultures learn the cognitive skills taught in Western schools, families and other settings, cognitive skills that are required for successful participation as adults in the occupational environment of Western industrial cities. (Ogbu, 1992, p. 369)

Most research that contributes to our knowledge base about developmental processes uses instruments and/or assessment tools that are standardized and validated in White middle-class populations or representative samples that include small groups from other races and ethnicities. Consequently, problems of validity, reliability, and interpretation arise when researchers employ these tools in other samples. To overcome this limitation, cross-cultural research has tried both to develop culture free tests and to be extremely cautious when interpreting scores obtained from standard tests (Segall, 1986). However, the creation of culture free tests has proven to be elusive if not impossible. Even performances on nonverbal tests that were at one point considered culture free have been proven to be sensitive to variances in the levels of exposure to representational art (Dennis, 1970).

The problem is not simply that tests created in one population are being employed in another, but also that from these constructs and assessment tools a single definition or standard of competence is created to which all other populations are compared (Azibo, 1988; Cole & Bruner, 1974; Ogbu, 1981). This reliance on culturally bound tools, tests, and assessment mechanisms to determine competencies blatantly disregards the fact that basic psychological and behavioral constructs might not mean in one culture what they do in another. As Matsumoto (1994) stated, "If a concept means different things to people of different cultures, then it is difficult to compare data on that concept across cultures" (p. 26). Matsumoto illustrates this problem with a discussion of the expression of intimacy across cultures. He explains that cultures have been found to express intimacy in different ways, largely because intimacy means different things in different cultures. If one culture defines intimacy by certain acts and another by shared psychological feelings the observation of different expressions of intimacy would reveal large difference across cultures. The critical issue for the researcher then becomes, does this concept mean the same thing in both cultures (Matsumoto, 1994).

A recent example of the creation of a culturally appropriate assessment tool is provided by our attempt to measure family values and functioning among Puerto Rican families in the United States (see Vázquez García, García Coll, Erkut, Alarcon, & Tropp, in press). A review of the extant instruments pointed out that fundamental constructs valued among traditional Puerto Rican families such as enmeshment in emotional functioning (Canino & Canino, 1980) and Familism or Respeto (Sabogal, Marín, Otero-Sabogal, VanOss Marín, & Perez-Stable, 1987) would be categorized as dysfunctional. This led us to the design and development of an instrument that defined the construct of family values and functioning with anchors and definitions based on traditional Puerto Rican values and traditions.

We operationalized the dimensions of Familism and Respeto found in the literature to include the following culturally specific factors: personal beliefs, family practices, and cultural precepts (what the person believes that the culture expects). Having done this we generated new items and adapted other items from previous scales. Examples of items generated to measure Familism were: "The family should consult with close relatives, uncles, aunts, grandparents its important decisions"; and "I don't want to bring up things I know my parents don't want to talk about." Items created to measure Respeto included: "People in my family are not comfortable hugging and kissing each other to show that they care"; and "Kids should not question adults" (see Vázquez García et al., in press).

Once the items were created several methods of translation were used to retain the linguistic integrity of the scale including the translation/back translation, decentering, and dual focus methods. Finally, we employed focus groups and individual interviews with adolescents and parents in five locations: New England, Puerto Rico, Panama, Guatemala, and Honduras. Following the feedback from the interviews and focus groups further revisions were made to drop some items, change some wording, and validate both the Spanish and English versions of the scale.

The final scale that was generated consisted of 29 items on a 7-point Lickert scale that measured Respeto and Familism. The scale was given to a group of 80 adolescent Hispanics who self-identified as Puerto Ricans, Mexicans, Salvadoran, Guatemalan, Nicaraguan, Dominican, Hispanic/Latino, among others. The sample included both adolescents who had been born in the United States and those who had migrated here.

The results showed that the adolescents had a higher adherence to Familism than to Respeto. Furthermore, those who had lived in the United States for a longer period of time scored higher on most of the scale's items, indicating less adherence to Familism and Respeto values than adolescents who had lived in their country of origin longer. The findings suggest that Hispanic adolescents' adherence to family values changes as a result of contextual demands including migration and acculturation. By using multiple methods of creation, investigation, and validation a culturally appropriate scale to assess the family values and functioning of Hispanic adolescents was created.

One last consideration in the area of measurement is that most of our methods and assessment tools assume context-free universal competencies. Our approach is to minimize the impact of environment: to control it, to standardize it, rather than to involve it as part of our assessments (Adomapaulos & Lonner, 1994). This approach arises from a conceptualization of development that separates developmental processes from the environmental contexts in which they occur. However, if we are interested in contextual influences on development, which is one way that cultural influences are operationalized, a different approach to our research is necessary.

An interesting example of how variations in context as part of the assessment of developmental competencies informs how culture affected development is represented by the pioneer work of Labov (1970). He examined speech patterns of inner city African American children as it related to a cultural deficiency theory which posited that children's speech development was hindered by an impoverished and verbally deprived early environment. He demonstrated that the concept of cultural or verbal deficiency was not based in social reality. Labov showed that while under one set of interview conditions (asymmetrical situation, large White male interviewer) a young African American boy seemed to have rather poor verbal capacity, that the same child facing different interview conditions (not asymmetrical, African American familiar interviewer) demonstrated a far greater verbal capacity. He concluded that "the social situation is the most powerful determinant of verbal behavior and that an adult must enter into the right social relations with a child if he wants to find out what a child can do" (p. 163). Had the interviewer not considered contextual influences, he could have inferred erroneously an incorrect competence level directly from the child's performance in a particular context.

More recently, Fisher, Bullock, Rotenberg, and Raya (1993) demonstrated the powerful effects of context on children's performance of cognitive tasks. By manipulating support (priming) they revealed the dramatic influence that contextual variables can have on a children's performance of both sorting tasks and story recreation. If the study of development is to shift to include cultural considerations at the core of its paradigm, it must at the same time acknowledge and account for contextual considerations and this requires that "behavior is studied not as something disembodied but within a matrix of body, emotion, belief, value, and physical world"(Wozniak & Fischer, 1993, p. xi).

ANALYTICAL METHODS

The consideration of cultural influences on development also require a careful examination of the assumptions made by our data analysis techniques. Basically, our high regard for and commitment to measurable and quantifiable variables requires that our hypotheses be supported by statistical evidence. However, the simultaneous consideration of multiple individual and contextual variables, as it would be required by the study of cultural influences on development, poses specific challenges to our traditional analytic methods.

In order to study cultural influences on development, the statistical analysis techniques must be able to appropriately consider multiple variables and their interactions simultaneously. The availability of multivariate statistics provides the opportunity to conduct such an inquiry, although these techniques require substantial sample sizes. A good example was provided by the exploratory analyses that we conducted in one of our studies of developmental outcome in infants of adolescent mothers (see García Coll, Vohr, Hoffman, & Oh, 1986, for complete details of the study) where we employed LISREL (Jöreskog & Sörbom, 1979, 1981) analysis techniques. Figure 1.1 shows the LISREL model that was hypothesized and

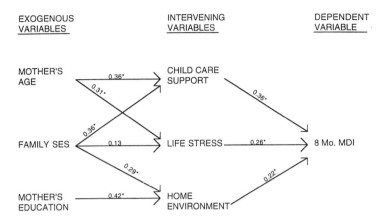

FIG. 1.1. LISREL causal model of maternal and environmental factors on 8-month MDI. From García Coll, Vohr, Hoffman, and Oh (1986). Reproduced with permission of *Journal of Developmental and Behavioral Pediatrics*, 7(4), 230–236.

tested empirically with data from Caucasian adolescent and adult mothers in Providence, Rhode Island.

We hypothesized that social address variables like the mother's age, her education, and the family socioeconomic background would influence developmental outcome indirectly through the mediating variables of childcare support, perceived life stress, and the quality of the home environment. Not only did this model account for a significant percent of the variance in the child's developmental outcome as measured by Bayley mental developmental indices (MDI) at 8 months of age, but an alternative model that tested direct pathways from the exogenous variables of age, education and SES did not improve the fit of the estimated correlation matrix nor did it reveal significant correlation coefficients relating these variables to the infant's MDI. In addition, we were able to specify that child care support and perceived life stress were the most important mediators to developmental outcome since the home environment coefficient failed to reach significance when the other variables were taken into account. The LISREL method was able to consider possible "cause" and "effect" relationships between a number of variable simultaneously, thus leading to a better understanding of the influence of a number of concurrent variables on the children's developmental outcomes.

However, even multivariate statistical methods make assumptions and require certain standards that might not be fulfilled when the complex questions about the dynamic interactions of developmental and cultural processes are asked. For example, in standard statistical analyses the two samples being compared need to have equal variances. However, in cross-cultural comparisons the distributions of variances might be different specifically because of the different cultural context being examined. In actuality, this difference in variances might be the most important window into the interplay of culture and developmental processes, and therefore our analysis techniques must employ methodologies that can recognize this important source of information.

Second, most of our statistical techniques that examine relationships among variables assume that these relationships will be linear, and while this might be true in one cultural context it is not necessarily true in all cultural contexts. Again this difference in the nature or direction of the relationships among variables might be an important consideration for the understanding of the phenomena under study.

Another important consideration is placed by the need to reduce the number of variables being analyzed to preserve an adequate ratio between the number of subjects and the number of variables being measured in a given study. Although this practice is necessary to maintain the integrity of the data analysis, the aggregation or simplification of variables might lead us to miss the complexity of the phenomenon we are attempting to understand. By combining variables that might differ in their associations across different cultural contexts the final analyses might lose some of the more subtle variations that exist within cultures.

Lastly, most of our statistical methods emphasize central tendencies rather than variability. In these methods, variability is deemed an error rather than a possible source of important information. Our statistical techniques might make us overlook the fact that cultural contexts might influence developmental processes by increasing or decreasing variability in the distribution of the phenomena under study. When differences in variances are found in a data set researchers should incorporate and address these findings in their interpretations and conclusions (Matsumoto, 1994).

An interesting alternative to the shortcoming of our statistical methods is presented by the use of qualitative and quantitative methods within the same research project. An interesting study that employs such an approach is Harwood's (1992) study of the influence of cultural values on maternal perceptions of infant attachment patterns. The investigation was composed of two steps. In the first part, the researcher used open ended inquiries to construct culturally relevant descriptors of desirable and undesirable Strange Situation behaviors. Having constructed these conceptualizations, comparative quantitative research was conducted that utilized the meaningful descriptors and vignettes in all three cultural groups. Thus, the study used an emic approach that mixed the best aspects of both quantitative and qualitative approaches.

Similarly, a study by Flanagan, McGrath, Meyer, and García Coll (1995) used a Grounded Theory method to examine adolescents' experiences of motherhood and to evaluate developmental influences on the concept of the maternal role within a group of predominantly poor minority women. First, qualitative methods were used to understand the specific phenomenon of how an adolescent experiences mothering in relation to her own development as an adolescent. Group and individual interviews were conducted with 42 poor minority teenage mothers, and the responses were analyzed for concepts and themes. A five question structured interview derived from the qualitative research was used in a second study to quantitatively test the correlations between responses on self-related and mother-related questions. The study revealed that adolescent mothers' experiences of motherhood and their conceptualizations of the maternal role was strongly related to their psychosocial cognitive development.

Another interesting study that demonstrates an alternative to traditional quantitative methods was conducted by Powlishta, Serbin, Doyle, and White (1994). In this study of prejudice in children, multiple quantitative methods are used across three different domains. Prejudice was measured through trait attribution, picture preference, social distance, and sociometric measures across the domains of gender, language, and body type. Thus, their work did not rely on one particular methodology nor on one particular domain. Furthermore a basic developmental competency in cognition, another area of development, was assessed and hypothetically related to attitude flexibility and prejudice, suggesting the importance of looking at the relationship among various areas of developmental competence.

Finally, the use of dynamic systems approaches to the study of developmental processes might provide another enlightening alternative to more traditional statistical methods (see Smith & Thelen, 1993; Thelen & Smith, 1994). These methods that are designed to deal with complexity, non-linearity, and context dependency have been applied successfully to the study of motor, perceptual, and cognitive development (see Smith & Thelen, 1993). This approach to studying development is useful because it relies on a more complex conceptualization of an organism. In this approach it is assumed that an organism is comprised of various subelements that change over time both individually and cumulatively. Consequently, the statistical methods based on dynamic systems approaches recognize that variations arise within and essentially because of the processes of development (Thelen, 1990) and consequently the study of variability becomes a major thrust of the investigation.

INTERPRETATION OF FINDINGS

The last important aspect of the proposed paradigm shift concerns the interpretation of the findings. The interpretation of any research findings reflect the theoretical framework that is guiding the study from its incep-

tion. Therefore, the choice and availability of a sound conceptual framework for the study of cultural influences on child development is a necessary
initial step in the proposed paradigm shift. There is a great need for theory
and construct development in this area (Cocking, 1992; García Coll et al.,
1996; Harkness, 1980). As Cole (1992) claimed:

> The task of specifying the mechanisms through which culture enters into
> the process of human development is seriously hampered both because
> currently dominant theories of development do not consider culture fun-
> damental to the process and because there are severe conceptual disagree-
> ments about the nature of culture even among anthropologists, for whom
> the concept is central. (Cole, 1992, p. 284)

Historically, most research on cultural influences of development have
not only used a comparative framework but have used deficit models to
explain the differences between the groups. Specifically, middle-class White
American standards have been used as the yardstick of success, and competence levels have been inferred directly from an individual's performance
on standardized tests or experimental procedures (Cole & Bruner, 1974).
The use of these models has hampered our ability to recognize the development of alternative competencies as a function of contextual demands (Cole
& Bruner, 1974; Cole, Gay, Glick, & Sharp, 1971; García Coll et al., 1996;
Ogbu, 1992) and precluded increasing our understanding of how culture
affects developmental processes (as exemplified by the work of Cole, Gay,
Glick, & Sharp, 1971; Labov, 1970; Ogbu, 1981, 1992, among others).

Even the results of research conducted within North American culture
caution us not to equate performance with capacity. Fisher, Bullock, Rotenberg, and Raya (1993) effectively argued that an individual's performance on standardized tests more often reflects a *skill* (improved performance through learning and practice in a particular context) rather than a
competency (underlying capacity). For this reason they argued that past
developmental theories which conceptualized competencies as independent of context and equated performance levels with ability were fundamentally flawed. They remind the researcher that caution must be used
when data is being interpreted because differences in performance do not
necessary reflect differences in competence.

A good example is provided by Rogoff and Waddell (1982), who looked
at the importance of equivalence of meaning in creating a task to measure
memory competencies as it related to interpreting competence levels. They
pointed out that in previous research, non-western populations have
showed deficits on list memory tasks, but that this deficit might reflect a
lack of western style schooling rather than an actual memory deficit. To
test their hypothesis they compared Mayan children with American chil-

dren on memory tasks that rather than using lists of objects employed miniature three dimensional scenes, in which familiar objects were specifically set, and then removed. The children were asked to recreate the scene, and as hypothesized, no memory deficit was found in the non-western population. Rogoff and Waddell's research involving contextually organized verbal information and spatial memory demonstrates that poor performance on list memory tests does not necessarily reflect a memory competency deficit.

Cole et al. (1971) suggested how a paradigm shift would change the framework that guides our study of competencies:

> If experiments are occasions to demonstrate the use of skills, then the failure to apply the skills that we assume are used in natural contexts becomes, not an illustration cultural inferiority, but rather a fact to be explained through study and further experimentation. We assume that in these cases, skills are available but for some reason the context does not trigger their use. We thus make ethnographic analyses prior to experimentation in order to identify the kinds of skills that often engage in and hence ought to be skillful at dealing with. (p. 217)

Thus the proposed paradigm shift would require that researchers acquire a thorough knowledge of the culture under study to inform all aspects of the investigation and especially the interpretation of the findings. This could be done through ethnographic work, actual membership within the culture, or collaboration with members of the culture and other knowledgeable individuals. It might require additional field work after the findings are obtained and particular caution in interpreting the findings.

SOME BATTLES ALREADY WON . . .

If we are serious about including cultural influences in our systematic study of developmental processes and incorporating these findings as part of our knowledge base about human development, in other words, if we are really ready to adopt the proposed paradigm shift, we do not have to start from scratch. Cross-cultural research has already shed light on some aspects of human development influenced by cultural processes and how these processes operate. A large percentage of this work has concentrated on cognitive processes like memory, including free recall, mathematical thinking, categorization, and successful completion of Piagetian tasks (Berry & Dasen, 1974; Nyiti, 1982; Posner, 1982; Rogoff & Wadell, 1982). The findings obtained from these studies has shifted our conceptualization of cognitive development from the acquisition of context free universal capacities to the development of cognitive skills (Mistry & Rogoff, 1994; Price-Williams, Gordon, & Ramirez, 1974). It has established the universality of these skills but also how they are closely tied to the context of practice (Cole et al., 1971). Researchers have come to recognize that performance does not necessarily represent an underlying ability but rather a learned skill in handling a particular situation, and that individuals are limited in their ability to transfer skills from one situation to another (Greenfield & Lave, 1982; Jahoda, 1986; Mistry & Rogoff, 1994; Rogoff, 1982).

This area of research has both uncovered and addressed the problems of using instruments and standardized methods developed in western industrial societies in cultures that might differ in their level of modernization, urbanization, and also their basic values (Dasen, 1994). Specifically, it has been replicated across many cultural settings that the familiarity of test materials and the meaning and relevance of the task presented has tremendous implications for an individual's performance (Mistry & Rogoff, 1994; Wagner, 1978).

For example, while examining the difference between formal and informal studying, Greenfield and Lave (1982) found evidence that performance on a task is affected by familiarity of the task and the materials presented. Their work combined the findings of their separate studies with tailors and their apprentices in Liberia and weavers and their apprentices in Mexico. In each study they presented the participants with a series of problems which varied in degree of similarity to the situations in which they learned either weaving or tailoring. For instance, the Liberian tailors and apprentices were asked to estimate the length of familiar objects, such as waistbands, and unfamiliar objects, such as wooden sticks. In both studies when the experimental tasks were similar in form to the tasks that were performed on a daily basis the tailors and weavers were able to bring their skills to bear on new problems and solve them successfully. However, Greenfield and Lave found that neither the weaving nor tailoring skills generalized very far beyond the circumstances to which they were ordinarily applied. Hence the tailoring experience was not nearly as helpful in estimating the length of a piece of wood as it was in estimating the circumference of trouser waistbands, and weavers were not as able to continue a novel pattern, as they were a recognizable one. Thus, the role of the cultural environment is to facilitate the development of specific cognitive skills (i.e., increase rate of acquisition in a particular domain), to determine the application of these skills in certain contexts and not others, and to promote the development and use of abstract, context free cognitive skills.

Although fewer studies have been conducted to examine the role of culture on the development of infant attachment, there is a rather substantial number using Strange Situation paradigm. Studies have been conducted in Germany, Japan, Israel, the Netherlands, Sweden, and Great Britain and their major findings shed light into the role of cultural influences on development. One of the main findings is that a majority of infants can be classified into the patterns observed in the United States. Specifically, the "B" classification (secure attachment) is modal in all countries (see Bretherton, 1985; van IJzendoorn & Kroonenberg, 1988). Thus, the construct of secure–insecure attachment as measured by the Strange Situation seems to have cross-cultural validity.

However, the proportion of infants classified into each group appears to be affected by cultural influences. In many of the countries studied, the percentage of infants classified as avoidant (A), secure (B), and resistant (C) is different from the observed percentage distribution of classifications in the United States (Bretherton, 1985; van IJzendoorn & Kroonenberg, 1988).

For example, a study in northern Germany had a higher percentage of its sample classified as avoidant than the "standard" for the United States, which is about 20% (van IJzendoorn & Kroonenberg, 1988). This finding has been attributed to the prevalent cultural pressures in Germany to begin independence training at an early age (Grossman, Grossman, Spangler, Suess, & Usner, 1985). Israel, Japan, and nonacculturated Chinese in the United States show a much higher percentage of infants classified as resistant and these findings have been interpreted as a function of the extreme stressfullness of the Strange Situation paradigm for individuals in societies that do not utilize nonfamily babysitters or have high levels of stranger anxiety (Bretherton, 1985; Miyake, Chen, & Campos, 1985; Sagi, Lamb, Lewkowicz, Shoham, Dvir, & Estes, 1985). As Bretherton (1985) suggested, "Cultural variations engender different experiences leading to different relationship patterns" (p. 25).

Another area of attachment affected by cultural context is maternal perceptions of attachment behaviors. In a recent study Harwood (1992) utilized both qualitative and quantitative approaches to determine mothers' perceptions of desirable and undesirable infant reactions to the Strange Situation. She found that mothers' perceptions of children's behavior in the Strange Situation varied across cultures. Specifically, the Anglo mothers, as compared to Puerto Rican mothers, placed significantly more value on the characteristics and behaviors associated with the development of personal abilities and less value on the three characteristics associated with the maintenance of proper respect and demeanor. Furthermore, even when both sets of mothers determined that the C1 classification was undesirable they differed on their explanations as to why it was undesirable. Puerto Rican mothers were more likely to emphasize the lack of ability of these children to maintain a calm and respectful demeanor and the Anglo mothers were more likely to highlight their inability to function autonomously. Thus, this study suggests that not only might the distribution of classifications vary across cultures but the perceptions of these behaviors might vary as well.

In contrast, the variance in the percentages of the distributions of attachment classification across cultures does not necessarily reflect different correlations among the variables. The relationships of maternal behavior with Strange Situation classifications in these cross cultural studies are similar to those obtained in the United States by Ainsworth, Blehar, Waters, and Wall (1978). Grossman et al. (1985) replicated Ainsworth's finding that linked early maternal sensitivity to secure attachment. They found that maternal responsiveness was associated with less infant distress. Furthermore, Li-Repac's research (cited in Bretherton, 1985) also found the same relationships between classification and maternal responsivity in his investigation of Chinese Americans.

The importance of these studies is in their demonstration of how culture can impact the study of development processes both across cultural groups and within cultural groups. In their review of attachment studies, van IJzendoorn and Kroonenberg (1988) revealed that intracultural differences are 1.5 times larger than cross-cultural differences. In particular, the aggregate distribution of the 18 different studies conducted in the United States is similar to the "global distribution" but the individual sample distributions vary widely from each other. One reason might be that the samples were selected from different strata within each populations. A study of middle-class professional families had different results from studies focusing on lower socioeconomic families. The authors point out that some of the studies conducted in the United States had distributions that were more similar to other foreign samples than to each other, leading them to conclude: "It is clear that great caution should be exercised in assuming that an individual sample is representative of a particular (sub)culture and that the eccentric status of an 'outlier' distribution should await replication before it is brought to bear on cross-cultural debates" (van IJzendoorn & Kroonenberg, 1988, p. 154).

CONCLUSIONS

The main thesis of this chapter is the proposal of a paradigm shift in order to effectively study the interplay of cultural and developmental processes. Unless the dominant research paradigm in developmental science allows the flexibility of thinking and methodology that this paradigm shift requires, the knowledge base of basic developmental processes will continue to exclude cultural influences. This omission can have very serious negative consequences because it will perpetuate the lack of knowledge about which processes are basically universal and which ones are culturally relative. Given the extensive economic, political, and ecological interdependence of our world, the limitations of our knowledge base will grow even more evident in the future.

The call for a paradigm shift is not superfluous. It is a necessary step in our scientific endeavors to reflect the reality of children's lives in our own country and around the world. Ultimately, science can not only increase our understanding of developmental processes, but can shape the context of development for children in effective ways. If that is one of our goals as developmental researchers, then we need to let go of some of our most dear theoretical and methodological assumptions. So the question remains. . . . *Are we ready for a paradigm shift?*

REFERENCES

Adamopoulos, J., & Lonner, W. J. (1994). Absolutism, relativism, and the universalism in the study of human behavior. In W. L. Lonner & R. Malpass (Eds.), *Psychology and culture* (pp. 129–134). Needham Heights, MA: Allyn & Bacon.

Ainsworth, M. D. S., Blehar, M. C., Waters, E., & Wall, S. (1978). *The patterns of attachment: A psychological study of the strange situation.* Hillsdale, NJ: Lawrence Erlbaum Associates.

Azibo, D. A. (1988). Understanding the proper and improper usage of the comparative research framework. *The Journal of Black Psychology, 15*(1), 81–91.

Betancourt, H., & López, S. R. (1993). The study of culture, ethnicity, and race in American Psychology. *American Psychologist, 48*(6), 629–637.

Berry, J. W., & Dasen, P. R. (1974). *Culture and cognition: Readings in cross-cultural psychology.* London: Methuen.

Bretherton, I. (1985). Attachment theory: Retrospect and prospect. In I. Bretherton & E. Waters (Eds.), Growing points of attachment theory and research. *Monographs of the Society for Research in Child Development, 50*(1–2, Serial No. 209), 3–35.

Canino, I. A., & Canino, G. (1980). Impact of stress on the Puerto Rican family: Treatment considerations. *American Journal of Orthopsychiatry, 50*(3), 535–541.

Chen, C., & Stevenson, H. W. (1989). Homework: A cross-cultural examination. *Child Development, 60*(3), 551–561.

Cocking, R. R. (1992). Ecologically valid frameworks of development: Accounting for continuities and discontinuities across contexts. In P. M. Greenfield & R. R. Cocking (Eds.), *Cross-cultural roots of minority child development* (pp. 393–409). Hillsdale, NJ: Lawrence Erlbaum Associates.

Cole, M. (1992). Culture and cognitive development: From cross-cultural comparisons to model systems of cultural mediation. In A. F. Healy, S. M. Kosslyn, & R. M. Shiffrin (Eds.), *From learning processes to cognitive processes: Vol 2* (pp. 279–305). Hillsdale, NJ: Lawrence Erlbaum Associates.

Cole, M., & Bruner, J. S. (1974). Cultural differences and inferences about psychological processes. In J. W. Berry & P. R. Dasen (Eds.), *Culture and cognition: Readings in cross cultural psychology* (pp. 231–246). London: Methuen.

Cole, M., Gay, J., Glick, J. A., & Sharp, D. W. (1971). *The cultural context of learning and thinking: An exploration in experimental anthropology.* New York: Basic Books.

Cooper, C. (1994). Cultural perspectives on continuity and change in adolescents' relationships. In R. Montemayor, G. R. Adams, & T. P. Gulotta (Eds.), *Advances in adolescent development: Vol. 6. Personal relationships during adolescence* (pp. 78–100). Newbury Park, CA: Sage.

Dasen, P. R. (1974). The influence of ecology, culture, and European contact on cognitive development in Australian aborigines. In J. W. Berry & P. R. Dasen (Eds.), *Culture and cognition: Readings in cross cultural psychology* (pp. 381–408). London: Methuen.

Dennis, W. (1970). Goodenough scores, art experience, and modernization. In I. Al-Issa & W. Dennis (Eds.), *Cross cultural studies of behavior* (pp. 134–152). New York: Holt, Rinehart & Winston.

Fischer, K. W., Bullock, D. H., Rotenberg, E. J., & Raya, P. (1993). The dynamics of competence: How context contributes directly to skill. In R. H. Wozniak & K. W. Fischer (Eds.), *Development in context: Acting and thinking in specific environments* (pp. 93–117). Hillsdale, NJ: Lawrence Erlbaum Associates.

Flanagan, P. J., McGrath, M. M., Meyer, E. C., & García Coll, C. T. (1995). Adolescent development and transitions to motherhood. *Pediatrics, 96*(20), 273–277.

García Coll, C. T. (1989). The consequences of teenage childbearing in traditional Puerto Rican culture. In J. K. Nugent, B. M. Lester, & T. B. Brazleton (Eds.), *The cultural context of infancy: Vol. 1* (pp. 111–132). Norwood, NJ: Ablex.

García Coll, C. T., Escobar, M., Cebollero, P., & Valcárcel, M. (1989). Adolescent pregnancy and childbearing: Psychosocial consequences during the postpartum period. In C. T. García Coll & M. de Lourdes Mattei (Eds.), *The psychosocial development of Puerto Rican women* (pp. 84–114). New York: Praeger.

García Coll, C., Lamberty, G., Jenkins, R., McAdoo, H. P., Crnic, K., Wasik, B. H., & Vázquez García, H. (1996). An integrative model for the study of developmental competencies in minority children. *Child Development, 67*(5), 1891–1914.

García Coll, C., & Vázquez García, H. A. (1995). Hispanic children and their families: On a different track from the very beginning. In H. E. Fitzgerald, B. M. Lester, & B. Zuckerman (Eds.), *Children of poverty: Research, health, and policy issues* (pp. 57–83). New York: Garland.

García Coll, C., Vohr, B., Hoffman, J., & Oh, W. (1986). Maternal and environmental factors affecting developmental outcome of infants of adolescent mothers. *Journal of Developmental and Behavioral Pediatrics, 7*(4), 230–236.

Goduka, I. V., Poole, D. A., & Aotaki-Phenice, L. (1992). A comparative study of Black South African children from three different contexts. *Child Development, 63*(3), 509–525.

Graham, S. (1992). Most of the subjects were White and middle class. *American Psychologist, 47*(5), 629–639.

Greenfield, P. M., & Lave, J. (1982). Cognitive aspects of informal education. In D. A. Wagner & H. W. Stevenson (Eds.), *Cultural perspectives on child development* (pp. 146–165). San Francisco: W. H. Freeman.

Grossman, K., Grossman, K. E., Spangler, G., Suess, G., & Unzner, L. (1985). Maternal sensitivity and newborns' orientation responses as related to quality of attachment in Northern Germany. In I. Bretherton & E. Waters (Eds.), Growing points of attachment theory and research. *Monographs of the Society for Research in Child Development, 50*(1–2, Serial No. 209), 233–256.

Harkness, S. (1980). The cultural context of child development. *New Directions for Child Development, 8*, 7–14.

Harwood, R. (1992). The influence of culturally deprived values on Anglo and Puerto Rican mothers' perceptions of attachment behavior. *Child Development, 63*, 822–839.

Holtzman, W. H., Díaz-Guerrero, R., & Swartz, J. D. (1975). *Personality development in two cultures: A cross-cultural longitudinal study of school children in Mexico and the United States.* Austin: University of Texas Press.

Hoshmand, L. T., & Polkinghorne, D. E. (1992). Redefining the science-prentice relationship and professional training. *American Psychologist, 47*(1), 55–66.

Jahoda, G. (1986). A cross cultural perspective on developmental psychology. *International Journal of Behavior Development, 9*, 417–437.

Jöreskog, K. G., & Sörbom, D. (1979). *Advances in factor analysis and structural equations models.* Cambridge, MA: ABT Associates.

Jöreskog, K. G., & Sörbom, D. (1981). *Lisel V: Analysis of linear structural relationships by maximum likelihood and least square methods.* Chicago: International Educational Service.

Kessen, W. (1993). A developmentalist's reflections. In G. H. Elder, Modell, J., & Parke, R. (Eds.), *Children in time and place: Developmental and historical insights* (pp. 226–229). New York: Cambridge University Press.

Labov, W. (1970). The logic of nonstandard English. In F. Williams (Ed.), *Language and poverty* (pp. 153–189). Chicago: Markham.

Levine, L., García Coll, C. T., & Oh, W. (1985). Determinants of mother–infant interaction in adolescent mothers. *Pediatrics, 75*(1), 23–29.

Levine, R. A. (1980). Anthropology and child development. *New Directions for Child Development, 8,* 71–86.

Levine, R. A. (1973). *Culture, behavior, and personality.* Chicago: Aldine.

Matsumoto, D. (1994). *Cultural influences on research methods and statistics.* Pacific Grove, CA: Brooks/Cole.

Mistry, J., & Rogoff, B. (1994). Remembering in cultural context. In W. L. Lonner & R. Malpass (Eds.), *Psychology and culture* (pp. 139–144). Needham Heights, MA: Allyn & Bacon.

Miyake, K., Chen, S. J., & Campos, J. J. (1985). Infant temperament, mother's mode of interaction, and attachment in Japan: An interim report. In I. Bretherton & E. Waters (Eds.), Growing points of attachment theory and research. *Monographs of the Society for Research in Child Development, 50*(1–2, Serial No. 209), 276–297.

Newson, J., & Newson, E. (1974). Cultural aspects of childrearing in the English-speaking world. In M. P. M. Richards (Ed.), *The integration of the child into a social world* (pp. 53–82). London: Cambridge University Press.

Nyiti, R. M. (1982). The validity of "cultural differences explanations" for cross cultural variation in the rate of Piagetian cognitive development. In D. A. Wagner & H. W. Stevenson (Eds.), *Cultural perspectives on child development* (pp. 146–165). San Francisco: W. H. Freeman.

Ogbu, J. U. (1981). Origins of human competence: A cultural-ecological perspective. *Child Development, 52,* 413–429.

Ogbu, J. U. (1992). From cultural differences to differences in cultural frames of reference. In P. M. Greenfield & R. R. Cocking (Eds.), *Cross-cultural roots of minority child development* (pp. 365–391). Hillsdale, NJ: Lawrence Erlbaum Associates.

Posner, J. K. (1982). The development of mathematical knowledge in two West African societies. *Child Development, 53*(1), 200–208.

Powlishta, K. K., Serbin, L. A., Doyle, A., & White, D. R. (1994). Gender, ethnic, and body type prejudices in childhood. *Developmental Psychology, 30*(4), 526–536.

Price-Williams, D., Gordon, W., & Ramirez, M. (1974). Skill and conservation: A study of pottery-making children. In J. W. Berry & P. R. Dasen (Eds.), *Culture and cognition: Readings in cross cultural psychology* (pp. 351–352). London: Methuen.

Rogoff, B., & Morelli, G. (1989). Perspectives on children's development from cultural psychology. *American Psychologist, 44,* 343–348.

Rogoff, B., & Waddell, J. (1982). Memory for information organized in a scene by children from two cultures. *Child Development, 53*(5), 1224–1228.

Sabogal, F., Marín, G., Otero-Sabogal, R., VanOss Marín, B., & Perez-Stable, E. (1987). Hispanic familism and acculturation: What changes and what doesn't? *Hispanic Journal of Behavioral Sciences, 9*(4), 397–412.

Sagi, A., Lamb, M. E., Lewkowicz, K. S., Shoham, R., Dvir, R., & Estes, D. (1985). Security of infant–mother, –father, and metapelet attachments among kibbutz reared Israeli children. In I. Bretherton & E. Waters (Eds.), Growing points of attachment theory and research. *Monographs of the Society for Research in Child Development, 50*(1–2, Serial No. 209), 257–275.

Sameroff, A. J., & Chandler, M. (1975). Reproductive risk and the continuum of caretaking casualty. In F. D. Horowitz, E. M. Hetherington, & S. Scarr-Salapatek (Eds.), *Review of child development research: Vol. 4* (pp. 187–244). Chicago: University of Chicago Press.

Segall, M. H. (1986). Culture and behavior: Psychology in global perspective. *Annual Review of Psychology, 37,* 523–564.

Slaughter-Defoe, D. T., Nakagawa, K., Takanishi, R., & Johnson, D. J. (1990). Toward cultural/ecological perspectives on schooling and achievement in African- and Asian-American children. *Child Development, 61,* 363–383.

Smith, L. B., & Thelen, E. (Eds.). (1993). *A dynamic systems approach to development: Applications.* Cambridge, MA: MIT Press.

Super, C. M., & Harkness, S. (1980). Anthropological perspectives on child development [Special issue]. *New Directions for Child Development, 8.*

Super, C. M., & Harkness, S. (1994). The developmental niche. In W. L. Lonner & R. Malpass (Eds.), *Psychology and culture* (pp. 93–99). Needham Heights, MA: Allyn & Bacon.

Thelen, E. (1990). Dynamical systems and the generation of individual differences. In J. Coloumbo & J. Fagan (Eds.), *Individual differences in infancy* (pp. 19–43). Hillsdale, NJ: Lawrence Erlbaum Associates.

Thelen, E., & Smith, L. B. (1994). *A dynamic systems approach to the development of cognition and action.* Cambridge, MA: MIT Press.

Triandis, H. C., & Heron, A. (Eds.). (1981). *Handbook of cross-cultural psychology: Vol. 4. Developmental psychology.* Boston: Allyn & Bacon.

van IJzendoorn, M. H., & Kroonenberg, P. M. (1988). Cross cultural patterns of attachment: A meta-analysis of the strange situation. *Child Development, 59*(1), 147–156.

Vázquez García, H. A., García Coll, C., Erkut, S., Alarcon, O., & Tropp, L. (in press). Family values of Latino adolescents. In F. A. Villarruel (Ed.), *Latino adolescents: Building upon Latino diversity.* New York: Garland Press.

Wagner, D. A. (1978). Memories of Morocco: The influence of age, schooling, and environment on memory. *Cognitive Psychology, 10*(1), 1–28.

Weisner, T. S., Gallimore, R., & Jordon, C. (1988). Unpacking cultural effects on classroom learning: Native Hawaiian peer assistance and child-generated activity. *Anthropology and Education Quarterly, 19,* 327–351.

Whiting, B. (1976). The problem of the unpackaged variable. In K. Riegal & J. Meacham (Eds.), *The developing individual in a changing world: Historical and cultural issues: Vol. 1* (pp. 304–309). The Hague, Netherlands: Mouton.

Whiting, B. B., & Whiting, J. W. M. (1975). *Children of six cultures: A psychocultural analysis.* Cambridge, MA: Harvard University Press.

Wozniak, R. H., & Fischer, K. W. (1993). Development in context: An introduction. In R. H. Wozniak & K. W. Fischer (Eds.), *Development in context: Acting and thinking in specific environments* (pp. xi–xvi). Hillsdale, NJ: Lawrence Erlbaum Associates.

Chapter 2

Multiple Selves, Multiple Worlds: Cultural Perspectives on Individuality and Connectedness in Adolescent Development

Catherine R. Cooper
University of California, Santa Cruz

Studies of culture and human development often compare individuals from different national or cultural groups on the basis of two global qualities: *individualism* and *collectivism* (Greenfield & Cocking, 1994; Markus & Kitayama, 1991; Triandis, 1995). These are often portrayed as mutually exclusive values, stable over time, and typical of individuals in each group. For example, the United States and Europe are considered individualistic cultures and Africa, Asia, and Latin America as collectivist or communal. Perhaps because of this categorical approach, culture is often considered separately from indicators of variation and change within groups, such as age, gender, occupation, employment, poverty, generation of immigration, education, ethnicity, or "race."

In recent years, the international scholarly community has been seeking ways to understand the role of culture in human development without overemphasizing or ignoring either psychological ("micro") or sociological ("macro") processes (Nurmi, Poole, & Seginer, 1995; Phinney, 1993; Trueba, 1991). Interdisciplinary efforts are now converging to integrate four levels of analysis: At the level of *individuals,* scholars are defining successful development as more than a solitary journey of exploration, autonomy, and emancipation from parents (Archer, 1992; Heath & McLaughlin, 1993). At the level of *relationships,* we are moving beyond viewing children's social and cognitive development as the transmission of values, knowledge, and other "social capital" from older experts to younger novices (Mehan, Hubbard, Okamoto, & Villanueva, 1995; Rogoff,

1990). Third, we are revising assumptions that *linkages across social contexts* such as families, schools, or peers operate best by matching or fitting together (Parke & Ladd, 1992). Finally, at the level of *social institutions,* we are moving beyond assumptions of unrestricted opportunities in school (Bordieu & Passeron, 1977; Chisholm, Büchner, Krüger, & Brown, 1990; Kroger, 1993). While traditional views endure in scholarly and popular discourse, they are increasingly enriched by cultural perspectives.

We are coming to understand culture as a key part of the interplay among individuals, relationships, social contexts, and institutions rather than as a monolithic force acting on individuals or as immutable psychological traits. Beyond any scholarly goals, however, the recent resurgence in worldwide intolerance of ethnic and cultural diversity has triggered a sense of purpose and even urgency in many scholars to understand cultural stability and change without stereotyping groups, while contributing to productive actions on behalf of children, families, and communities (Heath, personal communication, 1996). For these reasons, it is particularly timely for developmental scholars to turn to issues of culture and development. We have long focused on variability and change as well as stability in individuals, and, more recently in relationships and social contexts involving families, schools, and neighborhoods. We now seek to define normal development to include diversity in culture, ethnicity, socioeconomic status, gender, family composition, and national origin (García Coll & Magnuson, chap. 1, this volume).

This chapter is framed as a contribution to this emerging interdisciplinary and international dialogue. For the past 20 years, my colleagues, students, and I have investigated how both successful and vulnerable youth are challenged to forge identities that incorporate the values of their cultural and family traditions as well as those of the school, community, and workplace. The participants in our studies have included African American, Chinese American, Vietnamese American, Mexican American, Central American, Filipino American, Japanese American, Japanese, European American, and multiple-heritage youth and their families. In collaboration with colleagues and students, we have developed a theoretical model of *Individuality and Connectedness* and the role of experiences reflecting these qualities in adolescents' developing sense of self, identity, relationships, and academic and occupational competence.

To test and refine this model, we have developed several interrelated lines of empirical work, including new methodological approaches. In this chapter I draw highlights from these studies to make two arguments. The first is that our general conceptions of culture and development, most typically framed by the mutually exclusive concepts of individualism and collectivism, can be enriched by multidimensional models of culture tracing the interplay of individuality and connectedness among individuals, relationships, and institutions. More specifically, I argue that research, practice, and social policies involving adolescents in diverse cultural communities, including their families, schools, and youth-serving community organizations, also benefit from such perspectives on culture and development.

I begin with an overview of our recent theoretical work in linking cultural and developmental perspectives on Individuality and Connectedness, and how our original model has been strengthened by recent work in *Ecocultural theory*, the *Multiple Worlds model*, and *parallel designs*. Next, I illustrate our empirical and methodological progress with highlights from three studies conducted with colleagues and students and with participants from diverse ethnic, cultural, and socioeconomic communities. Finally, I close by considering next steps in theoretical, methodological, and empirical work in diversity and developmental science.

LINKING CULTURAL AND DEVELOPMENTAL PERSPECTIVES ON THE INTERPLAY OF INDIVIDUALS, RELATIONSHIPS, AND INSTITUTIONS

Since its inception, the theoretical perspective of our work has focused on the interplay between individuality and connectedness in the ongoing mutual regulation in relationships as a context for adolescent identity development. Rather than framing individuality and connectedness as mutually exclusive qualities, our model proposes that their interplay is a key mechanism in both individual and relational development (Cooper, 1988; Cooper, Grotevant, & Condon, 1983; Grotevant & Cooper, 1986, 1988; see Grotevant & Cooper, 1998, for a review of this program of research). We defined *individuality* in terms of processes that reflect the distinctiveness of the self. In language, for example, it is seen in patterns and modes of assertions, disclosures, and disagreements with others. *Connectedness* involves processes that link the self to others, as seen in acknowledgment of, respect for, and responsiveness to others.

In our early studies, we analyzed the conversations of families and peers of European American adolescents from middle-class communities, recorded in their homes and schools (e.g., Carlson, Cooper, & Spradling, 1991; Cooper et al., 1983; Grotevant & Cooper, 1985, 1986). These studies revealed that family discourse reflecting the interplay of individuality and connectedness was associated with the breadth and depth of adolescents' identity exploration and the extent of their role taking skill. We also found that adolescents' capacity to coordinate their sense of self and others in family relationships appeared to be carried into worlds beyond it, particularly in peer relationships (Cooper & Cooper, 1992).

Our original goal of understanding individuality and connectedness in adolescents' relationships and identity development continues, but our recent work focuses more directly on cultural issues in the interplay of identity, relationships, social contexts, and institutional opportunities and barriers, particularly as mediated by close relationships. To strengthen the capacity of our model to address these issues, my colleagues and I have built on three conceptual contributions of other scholars: Ecocultural theory (Weisner, Gallimore, & Jordan, 1988), the Multiple Worlds model (Phelan, Davidson, & Yu, 1991), and the parallel design (Sue & Sue, 1987). We next examine each of these perspectives.

Unpackaging Culture: Ecocultural Theory

Rather than viewing culture in terms of static and mutually exclusive categories such as individualism or collectivism, Eastern or Western, or other dichotomies, social scientists in many countries are increasingly investigating how individuals, families, communities, and cultures *each* develop through time (Skolnick, 1993). In doing so, these scholars are engaged in what anthropologist Beatrice Whiting (1976) first called "unpackaging the independent variable" of culture. As Weisner, Gallimore, and Jordan (1988) argued, "Culture is not a nominal variable to be attached equally to every child, in the same way that age, height, or sex might be. Treating culture in this way assumes that all children in a cultural group have common natal experiences. In many cases, they do not. The assumption of homogeneity of experience of children within cultures, without empirical evidence, is unwarranted . . . a similar error is to treat national or ethnic status as equivalent to a common cultural experience for individuals" (p. 328).

Among the dimensions proposed in the Ecocultural framework, my colleagues and I have found four to be especially useful, both for "unpackaging" culture and for tracing cultural aspects of adolescents' individual and relationship development. The most fundamental to ecocultural analyses are the everyday routines or *activity settings* in which children, adolescents, and families participate, such as mealtimes, household chores, sleeping patterns, doing homework, literacy practices, or selling in the marketplace. A second dimension involves the configurations of *personnel* or key relationships involved in daily life. For example, personnel included in an adolescent's definition of her family might include her parents, siblings, grandparents, cousins, and godparents as well as her friends, coach, favorite teacher, and minister. A third key dimension involves recurring patterns of communication or *scripts* for expressing universal human tasks. In our work on the interplay of individuality and connectedness, we have focused on verbal and nonverbal forms of guidance, planning, negotiation, and conflict resolution. Finally, the Ecocultural model highlights the role of *goals, values, and aspirations* held by family and community members.

Although most research using the ecocultural approach has focused on infancy and childhood (e.g., LeVine, 1988; Rogoff, 1990; Tharp & Gallimore, 1988), we have found it especially useful in studying families' adaptations in the transition from childhood through adolescence. In particular, we probed six domains in which family members articulate goals and aspirations for their children and adolescents: family roles, education, occupation, morality, health, and ethnic identity. Because this transition involves increasing mobility and interactions beyond the family, we also traced how adolescents move across family, school, peer, and community contexts, rather than between two contexts at a time, such as families and school, families and peers, or school and work. For this issue we have built on the Multiple Worlds model of Phelan et al. (1991).

Beyond "Two Worlds" Models of Contexts: The Multiple Worlds Model

Phelan, Davidson, and Yu (1991) first described the *multiple worlds* of family, school, and peer relationships of high school students, and how youth struggle to integrate their experiences across these worlds with their views of themselves. Phelan et al. (1991) defined the concept of *world* as the "cultural knowledge and behavior found within the boundaries of students' particular families, peer groups, and schools . . . each world contains values and beliefs, expectations, actions, and emotional responses familiar to insiders" (p. 53). Borders between worlds can be defined by psychosocial, sociocultural, socioeconomic, linguistic, or gender-based features. So in essence, each world functions as a culture and each can be unpackaged in its ecocultural dimensions. The challenge for adolescents and for scholars alike is to understand the process of navigating and negotiating across the cultural boundaries of daily life.

Phelan and her colleagues followed a group of adolescents from their first to second year of high school in Northern California. The students were selected to vary in gender, ethnicity, achievement, and immigration history rather than to represent particular demographic categories. In an extensive investigation, the research team used a series of open-ended interviews as well as observations of students, teacher ratings, and other sources. Phelan et al. (1991) described four prototypic patterns by which the students attempted to navigate across the borders between their high school, family, and peer worlds. Some students experienced smooth transitions across these boundaries, in which values and ways of behaving were compatible. Whether high or low achieving, these students appeared to experience congruence between the goals and expectations of parents, friends, and teachers and their own values. A second group of students occupied different worlds with regard to culture, socioeconomic status, ethnicity, or religion, but they appeared to find crossing borders between worlds "manageable." These students seemed able to adapt to mainstream patterns, yet return to home and community when with their peers. Still, those students who attempted such identities risked criticism from those in the disparate worlds who expected adherence to the conventions of each (Fordham & Ogbu, 1986). A third group of students seemed to occupy different worlds and found crossing borders more difficult, and the most vulnerable group experienced themselves as occupying different worlds and found the borders between them impenetrable.

In our work on individuality and connectedness, the Multiple Worlds model has enriched our conceptions of links from adolescents' developing identity to their family, peer, and school contexts. In particular, the concept of navigating across worlds defines individuals as active, an advance that Bronfenbrenner (1988) called for in ecological and contextual theories of development, including his own.

A central issue concerns how to understand the multiple worlds of culturally diverse adolescents without fostering stereotypes based on race, ethnicity, gender, social class, or country of origin, linking community-specific and cultural-universal insights (Cooper & Denner, 1998). To address these goals, we adapted Sue and Sue's (1987) conception of *parallel designs*.

Beyond Viewing Cultural Differences as Deficits:
Parallel Designs

McLoyd (1991) argued that research designs comparing minority with mainstream youth have fostered the interpretation of differences between cultural and ethnic groups in terms of deficits, thereby perpetuating negative stereotypes. This tendency has been exacerbated when research funding and media coverage portray youth who are at risk for crime, drug use, and early pregnancy as ethnic minorities (Spencer & Dornbusch, 1990). Likewise, Takanishi (1994) has traced the costs of "model minority" stereotypes of Asian and Asian American children from comparing them to European American children on measures of academic achievement.

In Sue and Sue's (1987) *parallel design*, researchers first identify potentially universal processes of interest to them, such as how older community members can guide youth in developing work and family roles. Second, researchers develop ways to measure these processes that are appropriate for each cultural community being studied. This has been called the *emic* approach (Pike, 1966), in which researchers describe a cultural community from insiders' meanings and perspectives, seeking to discover rather than impose definitions and basing evaluative criteria on standards of the community. For example, older siblings in many communities play a valued role as "the third parent," guiding younger brothers and sisters toward maturity. In contrast, an *etic* approach involves comparing communities from outsiders' vantage points with standardized or universal criteria. In the third step of the parallel design, scholars identify *similarities and differences* within and across cultural communities in how goals are defined and what factors contribute to *variation within each group* in their development. For example, variation in sibling caretaking practices has been found to reflect changes in families' residence and children's school involvement (Weisner et al., 1988).

In sum, our original model of Individuality and Connectedness has been enriched by Ecocultural theory, the Multiple Worlds model, and parallel designs. In recent years, we have worked extensively with each of these approaches, which are compatible and synergistic. In the next section, illustrative findings from three recent studies are presented. Taken together, they examine cultural perspectives on four levels: defining individual maturity, development in the context of relationships, linkages across social contexts, and institutional opportunities and restrictions. We carry forward insights from Ecocultural theory by examining activity settings, personnel, scripts, and goals and values; from the Multiple Worlds model, by tracing adolescents' navigating and negotiating across their multiple worlds; and from the parallel design, by framing our questions in terms of potentially universal processes and taking the time to define constructs and develop measures within each cultural community studied. For each study, we follow the logic of the parallel design to examine variation within cultural communities as well as similarities and differences across communities.

THREE STUDIES OF CULTURE, INDIVIDUALITY, AND CONNECTEDNESS

Study I: Familistic Values and the Communication of Individuality and Connectedness With Families and Peers in Late Adolescence

Although psychological theories often define personal maturity in terms of individualistic values of autonomy, self-reliance, and emancipation from parents, many cultural traditions accord a central role to *familism*, which can be defined as lifelong expectations to provide support and allegiance to one's family and community. In such traditions, younger people are expected to show respect and reticence with elders more than express their personal viewpoints. Likewise, their achievements or failures bring pride or shame to the family as a whole rather than signifying autonomy or independence (Haines, 1988).

Familistic values have attracted scholarly interest because they are often considered a key asset for ethnic minority families in the United States, especially under conditions of racism, immigration, or poverty (Harrison, Wilson, Pine, Chan, & Buriel, 1990). The costs as well as benefits of familism have also been assessed (Tienda, 1980). Research with Mexican American, Central American, and Cuban American adults has shown that norms of family support appear stable across several generations after immigration to the United States (Sabogal, Marín, Otero-Sabogal, VanOss Marín, & Perez-Stable, 1987). Similarly, values reflecting traditional Chinese, Vietnamese, and Filipino emphasis on family harmony, respect, and obedience to those in authority persist despite the scattering of extended families (Haines, 1988; Hong, 1989; Santos, 1983). Familistic values are also reflected in patterns of communicating and negotiating individuality and connectedness during adolescence. For example, decisions regarding young adults' educational, career, dating, and marital choices may be made by the head of the household in recently immigrated families.

As a step in examining cultural perspectives on adolescents' individual and relational development, my students and I investigated familistic values and patterns of communication in an ethnically diverse sample of college students (Cooper, Baker, Polichar, & Welsh, 1993). We were interested in exploring variation within cultural groups by looking at students' immigration histories, ethnicity, gender, and socioeconomic factors such as their families' education and employment. Earlier research suggested that adolescents with recent immigration experiences might endorse familistic values and communication patterns more than European American youth or those whose families had been in the United States for several generations. Thus, we looked for evidence of intergenerational stability and change by whether immigrant youth would attribute familistic values to their parents more than to themselves.

Reasoning that familistic values of respect might make adolescents' overt expressions of individuality rare, we used interview and survey methods rather than observing face-to-face conversations as we had done in our earlier studies of family discourse (e.g., Grotevant & Cooper, 1985). We began with focus group interviews with college students from a range of cultural communities (Steward & Shamdasani, 1990). In each case, undergraduate students on our team who were members of a particular ethnic community took leadership roles in recruiting participants and conducting the focus groups. In the group interviews, our staff showed students questions from earlier studies of familism and questions about family ethnicity and communication. On the basis of participants' suggestions, we revised these questions and added open-ended questions to our survey about adolescents' and family members' ethnicity, education, occupation, generation of immigration, and languages spoken to different family members. We also held focus groups following the survey data collection to compare our interpretations with their experiences.

Research Participants. The Northern California college students who took our survey described themselves with more than 30 different ethnic labels. They averaged 19 years of age. Findings presented here involve students describing themselves as of Mexican ($N = 96$), Vietnamese ($N = 38$), Filipino ($N = 56$), Chinese ($N = 58$), and European descent ($N = 145$); the remaining students included approximately 10% multiple-heritage youth. Most students in the first four cultural groups were children of immigrants, and many were themselves immigrants, including 27% of Mexican, 52% of Chinese, 50% of Filipino, and 84% of Vietnamese descent participants; only 5% of the European-descent students were immigrants. With regard to socioeconomic status, parents of Mexican-descent students had less formal education than parents of students in the other groups, although unemployment appeared highest among parents of Vietnamese students (see Cooper et al., 1994, for details of the study).

Familistic Values and Communication. Students rated the extent to which they and their mothers, fathers, and maternal and paternal grandparents agreed with a list of familistic values reflecting how much families are seen as sources of support and of obligation as well as a reference group for decision making (adapted from Sabogal et al., 1987). Students also characterized their expressions of individuality and connectedness with their parents, siblings, and peers, and how comfortable they felt discussing a range of topics with each person.

Variation Within Cultural Groups

Adolescents' responses suggested both cultural continuity and change in familistic values across generations. For example, in response to the statement, "Older siblings should help directly support other family members economically," Vietnamese and Chinese-descent students reported sharing their parents' strong endorsements, Filipino- and Mexican-descent students endorsed this value less than their parents, and European Americans reported sharing their parents' weak endorsements of this value. Although these findings may reflect the differing proportions of immigrants in each cultural group in our sample, the pattern is consistent with findings by Sabogal et al. (1987) of cultural stability and change in familistic values across generations of immigration.

Similarities Across Cultural Groups

Adolescents in all five cultural groups saw their parents as holding stronger expectations than they did to use the family as a reference group in decision making, as tapped by their responses to statements such as "Much of what a son or daughter does in life should be done to please the parents," reflecting a main effect of generation, $F(4, 307) = 11.35$, $p < .001$. A second similarity across groups was seen in students' reports of family communication: Students in all groups reported more formal communication with their fathers and more open communication and negotiation with their mothers, siblings, and friends. For example, students in all groups rated the statements, "This person communicates openly with me about their feelings" and "I discuss my problems with this person" as less true with respect to their fathers than with their mothers, siblings, or friends (see Figs. 2.1 and 2.2).

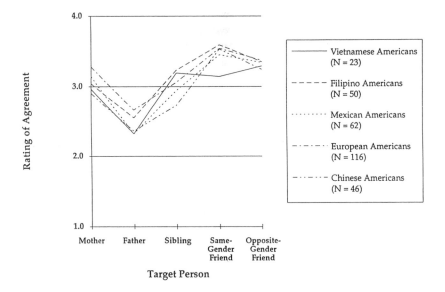

FIG. 2.1. Mean ratings by adolescents of the statement "this person communicates openly with me about their feelings" for family members and friends. From C. R. Cooper, H. Baker, D. Polichar, and M. Welsh (1993). Values and communication of Chinese, European, Filipino, Mexican, and Vietnamese American adolescents with their families and friends. In S. Shulman and W. A. Collins (Eds.), *Father–adolescent relationships: New directions for child development* (Vol. 62, pp. 73–89). San Francisco: Jossey-Bass. Adapted with permission.

I Discuss My Problems With This Person

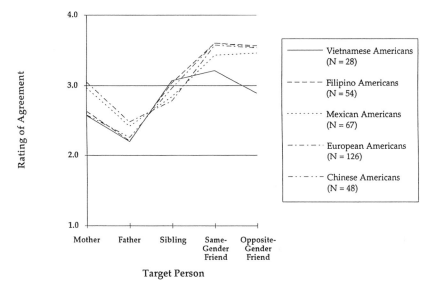

FIG. 2.2. Mean ratings by adolescents of the statement "I discuss my problems with this person" for family members and friends. From C. R. Cooper, H. Baker, D. Polichar, and M. Welsh (1993). Values and communication of Chinese, European, Filipino, Mexican, and Vietnamese American adolescents with their families and friends. In S. Shulman and W. A. Collins (Eds.), *Father–adolescent relationships: New directions for child development* (Vol. 62, pp. 73–89). San Francisco: Jossey-Bass. Adapted with permission.

Differences Across Cultural Groups

Mexican-, Chinese-, Vietnamese-, and Filipino-descent students endorsed the importance of turning to parents and other relatives in making important decisions and of mutual support among siblings more than the European-descent students in the sample. This finding was notable in relation to students' reports of how comfortable they felt talking with their fathers, mothers, siblings, and friends on two topics: sexuality, dating, and marriage; and how well they were doing in school. For each topic, students rated statements of the form "I feel comfortable talking about X with this person," with 1 = disagree, 2 = somewhat disagree, 3 = somewhat agree, and 4 = agree. As shown in Table 2.1, main effects of cultural group, relationship, and interactions were found for both topics. On the topic of sexuality, dating, and marriage, college students in all five cultural groups reported what we call a "gradient of comfort," feeling the least comfortable with their fathers and progressively more so with their mothers, siblings, and friends. Differences across cultural groups emerged as well: Chinese

TABLE 2.1
Adolescents' Comfort Levels When Talking With Family Members and Friends

I feel comfortable talking about sexuality, dating and marriage with this person.

Target Person	Vietnamese Americans (N = 24)	Filipino Americans (N = 42)	Mexican Americans (N = 63)	European Americans (N = 116)	Chinese Americans (N = 47)	Overall Mean* (N = 292)
Father	1.58	1.83	1.86	2.26	1.70	1.97[a]
Mother	1.88	2.12	2.52	2.81	1.98	2.44[b]
Sibling	2.92	2.74	2.76	2.99	2.51	2.82[c]
Same-Gender Friend	3.29	3.62	3.43	3.67	3.38	3.53[d]
Opposite-Gender Friend	2.96	3.64	3.44	3.57	3.36	3.47[d]
Overall Means**	2.53[e]	2.79[e,f]	2.80[e,f]	3.06[f]	2.59[e]	

I feel comfortable talking about how well I'm doing in school with this person.

Target Person	Vietnamese Americans (N = 24)	Filipino Americans (N = 42)	Mexican Americans (N = 63)	European Americans (N = 115)	Chinese Americans (N = 47)	Overall Mean* (N = 291)
Father	2.54	2.67	3.00	3.26	2.70	2.97[a]
Mother	2.79	3.02	3.22	3.41	2.85	3.17[b]
Sibling	3.08	3.12	3.18	3.30	3.30	3.23[b]
Same-Gender Friend	3.13	3.17	3.40	3.55	3.38	3.40[c]
Opposite-Gender Friend	3.13	3.31	3.41	3.56	3.49	3.44[c]
Overall Means**	2.93[e]	3.06[e,f]	3.24[e,f]	3.41[f]	3.14[e,f]	

*Rows with different letters (a–f) differ at the .05 level based on Newman-Keuls post-hoc tests.

**Columns with different letters (a–f) differ at the .05 level based on Newman-Keuls post-hoc tests.

Note. From C. R. Cooper, H. Baker, D. Polichar, and M. Welsh (1993). Values and communication of Chinese, European, Filipino, Mexican, and Vietnamese American adolescents with their families and friends. In S. Shulman and W. A. Collins (Eds.), *Father–adolescent relationships: New directions for child development* (Vol. 62, pp. 73–89). San Francisco: Jossey-Bass. Adapted with permission.

and Vietnamese American students in our sample reported feeling less comfortable discussing this topic than Filipino and Mexican American students, who in turn felt less comfortable than European American students. In absolute terms, Chinese and Vietnamese American students reported feeling somewhat uncomfortable discussing sexuality, dating, and marriage with their mothers, whereas Filipino, Mexican, and European American students, on average, reported feeling comfortable doing so.

On the topic of how well they were doing in school, students in all five cultural groups reported a similar comfort gradient, with progressively greater comfort beginning with fathers, then mothers, siblings, and friends. However, on the average, students in all groups reported feeling comfortable talking with their fathers about school matters. Besides illustrating the utility of the parallel design, these findings document the significance of topic in cultural analyses of communication.

Follow-Up Focus Groups

Following our survey, we held focus group interviews with students from each cultural group. We were particularly interested in asking students about what appeared to be a paradoxical finding: that students who held strong familistic values that they should turn to their families for advice on important decisions also reported that their communication with their parents, particularly their fathers, was sufficiently marked by respect, formality, and reticence that they were not likely to do so.

In these candid discussions, we talked with many students who confirmed holding familistic values and formal communication scripts with parents. They elaborated that they might discuss some topics involving school with their parents, but that their respect for parental authority might lead them to withhold more sensitive facts, such as having changed their undergraduate major from preparing for medical school (endorsed by their parents) to studying humanities or their exploring a gay sexual identity. Their comments indicated that negotiating personal identities and interpersonal jurisdiction continued to be salient issues of late adolescence (Yao & Smetana, 1993). Some students described conveying sensitive information to their fathers through intermediaries or brokers, most often their mothers, siblings, or cousins (Youniss & Smollar, 1985). Others described playing this broker role for their siblings; this role appeared more common among immigrant youth, several of whom saw themselves as "the third parent" in their families. Students were eloquent in describing how war, immigration, or poverty made their families much different than those portrayed in the research literature they were studying in their university classes, and these experiences were also reflected in relationships across the generations. As one Filipina immigrant student recalled:

I was with a single mother and I have one sister and it was really harsh . . . we basically did whatever (my mother) said, to keep the family alive. . . . But in terms of family values she would encourage family first—since this is the family that is giving you support, you need to be loyal to it and respect authority . . . I grew up with a lot of conflict with her . . . she wanted me to do really well in school but she didn't understand that those extra-curricular things you have to do to get into college mean taking you out of the home . . . I think because she was so much on her own, she knew what it took to survive and she wanted to make sure that I survived too. There was a lot of pressure on us to make sure we do well. We are like representatives of this family. Right now my mom and I are really good friends and I think the reason is my awareness of her life. . . . She started listening to the things that I was agreeing with and I said, "a lot of the things that I do is because of the values that you taught me . . . loyalty and respect for people, to be caring and giving." So it's funny, I've kind of impacted her now.

During the focus groups, students remarked that they discussed the challenges of coordinating family, career, and personal lives with their friends in ethnic student organizations. Said one student, "that's why we're involved with student groups." Although they felt they could talk to their parents about their goals more than when they were younger, their friends and student organizations played key roles during their college years.

Summary

Our findings regarding cultural patterns in values and communication reflecting individuality and connectedness challenge us to expand our definitions of adolescent maturity beyond individualistic qualities such as autonomy, self-reliance, and emancipation from parents to include enduring family responsibilities and norms of communication. Our study points to *variation within cultural groups* in terms of both continuity and change in familistic values and communication patterns. The importance of consulting families on major decisions and supporting siblings may decline over generations but these values also appear to persist over generations, a finding consistent with previous research with adult samples (Sabogal et al., 1987). *Similarity across cultural groups* was seen in our finding that communication appeared more formal with fathers than mothers in adolescents from all groups, whereas *differences* across groups were reflected in Chinese, Filipino, Mexican, and Vietnamese-descent students seeing themselves and their parents as holding stronger familistic values and more hierarchical communication, especially Chinese and Vietnamese American youth. In these families, when values of respect rendered adolescents' relationships with parents more formal, sibling and peer relationships appeared to play important roles, particularly on sensitive topics.

Among the limitations of using questionnaires, even in combination with focus groups, was that we could not interview adolescents or parents in detail. Nor could we examine experiences associated with immigration or poverty systematically, since they covaried in this sample. We pursued these issues in the following study of aspirations and guidance in low-income Mexican American and European American families during their children's transition into adolescence, for which we developed open-ended and qualitative methods to supplement quantitative approaches.

Study II: Aspirations and Guidance in Low-Income Mexican American and European American Families in the Transition to Adolescence

Educational difficulties of low-income students from diverse ethnic groups are often portrayed as stemming from "cultural mismatches" between families and schools, particularly in families' goals, aspirations, and patterns of guidance (Cazden, 1988; Heath, 1983). Low-income parents are often seen as holding low educational and vocational aspirations for their children that in turn contribute to school failure, unemployment, and persistent poverty. Yet recent work with low-income families has found that many parents hold high aspirations for their children but lack the institutional knowledge with which to guide them (Heath, 1983; Reese, Gallimore, Goldenberg, & Balzano, 1995). To investigate these issues, my colleagues Margarita Azmitia, Eugene García, and I, together with our students Lourdes Rivera, Rebecca Martínez-Chávez, Angela Ittel, Edward Lopez, and Nora Dunbar, examined the linkages between families and schools during the transition from childhood to adolescence (e.g., Azmitia, Cooper, García, Ittel, Johanson, Lopez, Martínez-Chávez, & Rivera, 1994; Azmitia, Cooper, García, & Dunbar, 1996; Cooper, Azmitia, García, Ittel, Lopez, Rivera, & Martínez-Chávez, 1994).

This program of research has involved two cultural groups in our community whose circumstances are of theoretical and policy interest. Mexican American families represent the largest group of immigrants in the United States. Although they experience high rates of unemployment, poverty, and school dropout (García, 1992), recent studies reflect growing scholarly interest in their educational achievement, occupational mobility, and strengths (Delgado-Gaitan, 1993; Gándara & Osugi, 1994), considering them as "at promise" as well as "at risk." In our study, we focused on parents born in Mexico whose children were born in the United States, many of whom have immigrated so their children's education will allow them to move out of poverty (Suarez-Orozco, 1991).

We chose our second group, low-income European American families, to contribute to cultural perspectives on this understudied community.

European Americans comprise the majority of the poor (such as those on welfare rolls), yet they are missing from discussions of poverty and developmental risk (McLoyd & Flanagan, 1990). Low-income European American parents' pessimism toward schooling as a way out of poverty has been implicated in their children's problems with school (Heath, 1983).

As with the previous study on familism and communication, we built on the Ecocultural model and parallel design to explore variation in each cultural group—in this case, in parents' aspirations and guidance during the transition to adolescence, as well as similarities and differences across groups, since relying solely on group differences may foster misperceptions that one is deficient relative to the other. As part of the study, we asked parents of third-, fifth-, and seventh-grade children about their educational, vocational, and personal–moral goals and aspirations and how they were helping their children attain them.

We were especially interested in age-related patterns in parents' aspirations and how their expertise across domains was reflected in their guidance. Age-related differences in parents' strategies might be influenced by their changing beliefs about children's development (Goodnow & Collins, 1990), such as giving older children greater responsibilities in planning their educational and vocational futures (Smetana, 1988). We explored evidence of such a shift among low-income families accommodating to a new culture or to a poverty niche.

Differential shifts over time may occur in parents' aspirations across educational, vocational, moral, health, or other domains. Parents might retain moral goals for older children while lowering their educational and vocational aspirations in response to teachers' evaluations (Erickson & Schultz, 1982; Goldenberg, Reese, Balzano, & Gallimore, 1993). They might place higher priority on immediate financial problems by asking older children to stay home to care for younger siblings or work to help the family. Or parents' fears for their children's safety might lead them to keep children home from school, thus superseding their educational and vocational goals.

Our staff interviewed members of 72 low-income families, 36 Mexican American and 36 European American families, whose children were receiving free or reduced-fee public school lunches. Equal numbers of children participated from each cultural group and gender at third, fifth, and seventh grades. The families lived in two small neighboring cities in central California, one an agricultural community of about 30,000 and the other a small coastal city of about 50,000.

The Mexican American families in the study had immigrated from rural areas of the Mexican states of Michoacán and Jalisco. Most families were headed by two parents, who had an average of 3 children. Parents worked as farm laborers or in canneries, although many were concerned about their jobs because canneries and food processing plants in the area were moving—ironically—to Mexico. Most parents were literate in Spanish but not English and had not gone beyond elementary school (*primaria*) in rural Mexico. Their poverty appeared long-standing; many had lived for several years in trailers or labor camps and their homes were generally small and sparsely furnished. Parents feared drug dealers and gang violence in their neighborhoods.

Among the European American families in the sample, most were headed by single parents, with fewer than 2 children on average. Most fathers and one third of mothers were employed, primarily as skilled manual workers, craftspersons, clerical or sales workers, or houseworkers. All were literate in English, with most having finished high school in the United States and many, some junior college. The onset of poverty for most of these families had been recent, typically resulting from divorce. Most lived in middle- or working-class neighborhoods they saw as relatively safe except for traffic. The remaining families were experiencing more pervasive poverty, with five being long-time residents in a neighborhood with affordable rents but also drug trafficking, prostitution, and gangs, and two having been homeless.

Parents were interviewed in their homes, with all but one of the Mexican American parents interviewed in Spanish by native speakers on our staff. In this study, interviews allowed participants to explain and elaborate their responses to our questions and were particularly important for parents with modest literacy skills. Following the Ecocultural dimensions, the interview focused on the *personnel* involved in the *activity settings* of chores and homework; parents' *guidance scripts* in each setting; and parents' long-term *goals, values, and aspirations* for their child's educational, occupational, and moral–personal maturity. Parents were asked open-ended questions for each domain, particularly about their goals and how they were helping their child attain them. Presented here are qualitative analyses of parents' responses to open-ended questions about their long-term aspirations and guidance; for details from the larger study, see Azmitia et al. (1994, 1996) and Cooper, Azmitia, et al. (1994).

Mexican American Families

Parents' aspirations and guidance appeared to differ between those of younger and older children in educational and vocational domains but not in the moral–personal domain. This finding may reflect parents' varying expertise across domains, their changing hierarchies of goals, and their response to neighborhood conditions with greater potential for straying away from the good path or *buen camino.*

Parents of third graders held educational and vocational goals that expressed their hopes of moving out of poverty and the dreams that motivated their immigration. They recounted telling their children to stay in school and out of trouble and describing what would happen if they did not, by using themselves and others as examples. One parent recalled, "Once it was still 4:30, so the men were in the fields picking artichokes and I said, 'You see, *mijo* (my child), that's a tough job. Day after day until the sun goes down they have to be out there—if it's hot or cold. Yes, *mijo*, that is why you guys need an education, because if you guys don't get enough education, you won't qualify for another job and you will be doing that for a living'. . . . I don't know if at his age it will stick, but hopefully it will."

Parents of fifth graders also emphasized the importance of their children staying in school, but some were ambivalent about these goals and despaired as to how they could help. They were less likely to mention professional occupations, saying they would be content with their children becoming secretaries, mechanics, or clerks. Some indicated that children should take responsibility for achieving their educational and occupational goals. As one parent said, "Well, I have the dream that he be somebody, but he still needs to put his share into this."

Parents of seventh graders tended to express lower educational and vocational aspirations than parents of younger children. Only a few mentioned college, and for some, even high school was in doubt. The theme that children should choose their own occupations was more prominent. Many said that as long as their children did not work in the fields or the cannery, any job would be fine. One parent said, "I would like her to get to college . . . but the way things are now, who knows?" This lack of planning may also reflect gaps between parents' and children's skills (Eccles, Midgley, Wigfield, Buchanan, Reuman, Flanagan, & MacIver, 1993). Parents with an elementary school education might have felt less qualified to plan their adolescents' educational and career future in a new culture with unfamiliar schools and occupations.

In the moral domain, parents of adolescents resembled those of younger children in emphasizing respect, honesty, responsibility, being a good person despite being poor, and in providing modeling and direct guidance. Said one parent, "we are people who are very poor, but we don't give them bad examples about anything. We behave well, hoping that they will learn to behave. If they see that we behave and are good persons, hopefully they will do the same."

European American Families

Although European American parents of third-grade students expressed a range of educational and vocational aspirations, their moral aspirations were consistently high. Some had devoted a great deal of effort to planning their children's future, whereas others had not done so but were helping their children attain their personal and moral aspirations. As one parent remarked, "I haven't thought about it too much. Education is not a big priority. It is more important that kids be emotionally healthy and happy. . . . I'm looking at the possibilities (for educational and vocational goals) and helping them learn to choose for themselves." Even parents who expressed high aspirations remarked that the future seemed beyond their control (Rodman & Voydanoff, 1988).

Many parents of fifth graders also saw educational and occupational aspirations as their children's choice. Some expressed doubts about their capacity to guide their children, although they linked both education and vocational domains to moral goals. One parent said, "I'm not one who dreams about my child's future. I still feel lost in trying to find *my* future. But I hope that he'll value education. And that he'll become educated just because of that's what you need in life, whether it applies to your job or not." Others expressed confidence in guiding their children toward the future, although in general terms. Said one, "I would like her to complete high school, and at least four years of college. . . . When I grew up a high school diploma was a real important thing. Now in this day and age a high school diploma doesn't mean beans. You've gotta have college. . . . The fact that I went back to school is a big help for her. (I) also take her going on some cleaning jobs with me and actually knowing how hard it is (the mother cleaned houses for a living). . . . I told her the more education you get, the more money you get and the easier the job is."

Parents of seventh graders held high aspirations for their children's moral and personal development and concern about their children's safety and staying on "the good path." Many saw education as a way to protect them from drugs and from becoming prostitutes. Helping with educational and vocational goals seemed to have been triggered by their adolescents' interests. One parent bought anatomy coloring books for a daughter interested in a medical career, while another found volunteer opportunities at the SPCA for a son hoping to be a veterinarian. Unlike the low-income families in Heath's study (1983), these parents did not question the value of education but rather the quality of their children's schools. This pattern may also reflect parents' viewing adolescence and young adulthood as the key time for career development (Goodnow & Collins, 1990).

Similarities and Differences Between Mexican American and European American Families

Mexican American and European American parents held similarly high educational aspirations for their children. Consistent with Reese et al. (1995), most Mexican American parents in the sample also held high professional aspirations for their children, with many hoping their children would become doctors, lawyers, or teachers. As one Mexican American parent said, "We aren't here (in the U.S.) because we like working here or like to live here. . . . We live better in Mexico. But I make this sacrifice because I want them to study, to learn English." However, more Mexican American parents were content for their children to finish high school, while more European American parents hoped their children would attend graduate school, although they often allowed their children to choose their level of education and occupational aspiration. Said one European American parent, "I don't want to impose anything on him, but I do tell him he has to study. I don't tell him he has to study such and such because I like it . . . I just want him to study a short career so that he has a future."

Mexican American parents were more likely to report using *indirect* guidance such as by providing encouragement or support, using their own lives as examples of the costs of a poor education, or enlisting siblings and relatives to help, than *direct* guidance such as tutoring. Although parents in both groups saw themselves helping their children by offering encouragement, help, advice, and tutoring, Mexican American parents were more likely to describe using themselves as *negative role models* by telling their children not to work in the fields or cannery as they did. As one parent said, "anything as long as it isn't in the fields. . . . When I was very young I started to pick strawberries and I wouldn't want him to do that." Although European American parents also used their lives as models, their examples were more positive, telling children how they were trying to correct past mistakes such as dropping out of school or marrying too young, by earning high school equivalency degrees and enrolling in community college to attain their own career goals. Parents who were students saw their study habits as models for their children.

Parents in both groups hoped their children would be morally upright persons, respect others and themselves, and stay away from drugs, gangs, and other "vices." Especially striking was parents' determination to keep children on the good path or *buen camino* (Reese et al., 1995). As detailed by Azmitia et al. (1994), parents in both groups provided direct tutoring and explicit advice in the moral domain, saw themselves as experts, and used their lives as examples of values they hoped their children would exhibit as adults.

Summary

In both cultural groups, parents' aspirations and guidance appear to differ across educational, occupational, and moral domains and, in some cases, to differ between childhood and adolescence. The Mexican American parents saw education as a way out of poverty, yet also feared potential dangers in junior high school or that their children's advanced education might distance them from their families and communities. Like Reese et al. (1995), even though parents held high aspirations for their children, some did not know these goals required a college education, while others who sought college education for their children were unsure about application and financial aid. Parents of fifth and seventh graders appeared to hold lower educational and vocational aspirations than those of third graders and, to a greater extent, viewed their children's success as their own responsibility. This may reflect the fact that by fifth grade, many children in the sample had exceeded their parents' schooling and thus parents felt less able to help them. Other parents feared dangers in the neighborhood or school might lead their children away from the good path or *buen camino*, and saw protecting children from these dangers taking priority over other goals. Said one parent, "I have seen with other people that their children spend years in school and for what? All they learn are vices, and in the end, they no longer feel comfortable in our community and then they aren't comfortable anywhere, at home or at school." The reality of these threats was reflected in the occurrence, during our study, of several drive-by shootings in the community and the assault and murder of the older sister of one of our participating children in a schoolyard.

The European American parents in the sample expressed high aspirations, but some were skeptical that schools could help their children acquire skills they needed to succeed, whereas others worried whether they had the financial or emotional resources to guide their children toward maturity. Unlike the parents of third and fifth graders, parents of seventh graders were actively guiding their children's educational and vocational aspirations, apparently triggered by their adolescents' formulating their educational and vocational interests. Some recently divorced parents acknowledged they were more preoccupied with immediate concerns such as paying rent, completing homework, or dealing with children's misbehavior than with long-term vocational and educational dreams. Other vulnerabilities were indicated by fear or ambivalence toward school expressed by some parents in the sample, particularly those of adolescents.

The cross-sectional design of this study did not differentiate age-related shifts from cohort effects. Older children's lower fluency in English or their greater responsibilities for work and child care might have affected their schooling. We are now completing a longitudinal study following a larger sample of higher- and lower-achieving Mexican American and European American fifth graders from elementary school into junior high or middle school, based on interviews with parents and children, classroom observations, and teachers' ratings of children's and parents' academic involvement (Azmitia & Cooper, 1997). Through this program of research, we have come to view as inadequate the widespread conceptions of family–school linkages in terms of global cultural "matches" or "mismatches." Given the challenges of guiding adolescents through school experienced by families in many cultural groups, we now consider how individuals, relationships, and institutions can bridge across adolescents' multiple worlds.

STUDY III: BRIDGING ADOLESCENTS' MULTIPLE WORLDS OF FAMILY, SCHOOL, NEIGHBORHOOD, AND WORK

In many industrial countries, adolescents' route through school to occupational achievement has been idealized as a smooth "academic pipeline," with access by choice and advancement through merit and individual effort. However, this view may be inappropriate for youth who encounter ethnic, racial, gender, economic, or political barriers to access, choice, and advancement. Recent research indicates that as each age cohort of students moves through secondary school and university in the United States, the percentage of ethnic minority adolescents shrinks (O'Brien, 1993), with similar patterns reported in other nations (Chisholm et al., 1990).

Explanations of these patterns have focused on concepts of *cultural capital* and *oppositional identity*, suggesting that students with more resources (such as parental education) and fewer structural barriers (such as racism, sexism, and other restrictions that discourage personal agency) would achieve at higher levels (Coleman, 1988; Ogbu, 1991). As we discussed in the previous study of low-income Mexican American and European American families, parents may hold high educational and vocational aspirations for their children, but those with less formal education may lack knowledge about schools, and those with histories of immigration or minority status may lose confidence that schooling is accessible or even beneficial to their children.

Our perspective, based on the Individuality and Connectedness model, would predict that challenges can, under conditions of support, facilitate adolescents' identity development and their motivation to succeed on behalf of their families and communities (Cooper, Jackson, Azmitia, Lopez, & Dunbar, 1995; Grotevant & Cooper, 1986). To do this, youth and their families may benefit from institutions and relationships that bridge from family to school and work, both to foster a sense of challenge and the skills to succeed.

In a collaborative investigation of this bridging process among individuals, relationships, and institutions, Jacquelyne Jackson, Margarita Azmitia, Robert Cooper, and I, together with our students Edward Lopez, Nora Dunbar, and July Figueroa, worked with the leadership and staff of university academic outreach programs that provide such bridging through school into college and college-based occupations. Our team built on the Multiple Worlds model of Phelan et al. (1991) to examine the experiences of African

American and Latino junior high, high school, and college students participating in the Mathematics, Engineering, Science Achievement Program (MESA), the Early Academic Outreach Program (EAOP), and Upward Bound. In the larger project, we assessed the perspectives of adolescents, parents, and outreach program staff so we could examine links between such relationships and students' academic achievement and career identity development. We did not conduct formal program evaluations, which fall within the scope of other research (e.g., Edgert & Taylor, 1992).

Following the parallel design, we conducted an initial study, in which we interviewed directors and staff about the histories of the programs and their current circumstances, observed in the programs, and conducted a series of six focus groups with junior high, high school, and college students grouped separately by gender, with approximately equal numbers of African American and Latino students in each group (for details see Cooper, Jackson, Azmitia, Lopez, & Dunbar, 1994; Cooper, Jackson, Azmitia, Lopez, & Dunbar, 1995). We developed a set of open-ended questions, adapted from the interviews of Phelan et al. (1991) and Weisner et al. (1988): What are your main worlds? What do you usually do in each world? Who are the main people in each of your worlds? What do people in each world expect you to be? What do *you* want to be? How do your worlds fit together for you? Which feel separate? Which feel as though they overlap? How does being your ethnicity and your gender affect your experiences in these worlds?

Worlds and Personnel. In the focus groups, students at each age level readily discussed and drew a wide array of worlds in their lives, including their families, their countries of origin, friends' homes, churches, mosques, academic outreach programs, shopping malls, video arcades (reported by most junior high school boys and no girls), school clubs, and sports. Over half the students described more than one family world. Students spontaneously referred to people in their academic outreach programs as like family and their fellow students as like brothers and sisters, listing them as family members, while listing brothers and sisters as resources at school.

Communication Scripts and Expectations. Both African American and Latino students described communication scripts and expectations across their worlds. Two scripts were especially relevant to navigating the academic pipeline: Students detailed experiences of *gatekeeping*, when teachers and counselors discouraged them from taking math and science classes required for university admission or attempted to enroll them in non-college tracks. Students also recounted negative expectations they had experienced from each of their worlds. Schools and neighborhoods were the greatest sources of students' expectations that they would fail, become pregnant and leave school, or engage in delinquent activities.

Students also described *brokering* by families, program staff, teachers, siblings, and friends providing support or speaking up for them at school, home, or neighborhood worlds. The academic outreach programs provided students not only with high academic expectations but also with a sense of moral goals to do "something good for your people," such as working as engineers in their communities and helping younger siblings attend college. Students also felt support retaining goals for academic success and ties to friends in home neighborhoods who were not in school or were affiliated with gangs.

On the basis of our focus groups, we developed the Multiple Worlds Survey (Cooper, Jackson, Azmitia, Lopez, & Dunbar, 1994). On the survey, students describe their worlds, who is in each world, expectations held by people in each world, and who helps and causes difficulties with schoolwork, with math, keeping up with responsibilities, feeling confident, and with sexism and racism.

We recently conducted a larger study of the resources and challenges experienced by African American and Latino youth in their worlds of family, school, and peers (Cooper, Jackson, Azmitia, Lopez, & Dunbar, 1995). Based on Ecocultural and Multiple Worlds theories, we focused on key personnel and communication scripts involving resources (who helps) and challenges (who causes difficulties) in each world. We also assessed the association between students' resources and challenges and their academic competence; based on the significance of math grades for college admission, we used them to index academic competence for the analyses reported.

From a larger sample of students in the Mathematics, Engineering, and Science Achievement (MESA) and the Early Academic Outreach Program (EAOP), we analyzed survey responses from 60 African American and 60 Latino students in Grades 6–12, including 30 males and 30 females in each cultural group. African American students in the sample were primarily born in the United States. Most of their parents had attended college and worked in middle-class occupations. Latino students in the sample were primarily born in the United States. Most of their parents were immigrants, primarily from Mexico, in middle- and working-class occupations. About one third of the mothers and fathers had attended college and about the same proportion had schooling at junior high level or below.

Personnel and Communication Scripts. Students named their mothers and fathers most frequently as resources, especially in helping them keep up with responsibilities, stay on track to college, and helping with sexism and racism. Some fathers caused difficulties planning the future, and some mothers caused difficulty with finances. Students named teachers as providing help and encouragement in math, and also as sources of difficulties with sexism and racism. Peers were the most controversial persons in students' lives: they were resources in helping students feel confident and special and in speaking up for them at school, yet peers were also the greatest source of difficulties with schoolwork, feeling confident, keeping up with responsibilities, and with sexism and racism. Self-governance was an unexpected theme in students' responses, as shown by students spontaneously naming themselves as sources of help with most scripts and as sources of difficulty in keeping up with responsibilities.

Links to Adolescents' Academic Competence. Although most students in the sample were relatively successful at school, we differentiated *higher achievers*, with average math grades of 3.7 or more (where a grade of A = 4.0), from *lower achievers* with average grades of 2.0 or less. Each group included 30 students, with equal numbers of African American and Latino, and of males and females and a modal level of 10th grade (15 years old). For each script (for example, "who helps you with math?") we computed chi-square statistics to compare higher versus lower achievers and students who did versus those who did not cite a particular person as helping with that script. For each finding cited, $X^2(1)$, $p < .05$.

Students making higher math grades were more likely than lower-achieving students to name their mothers and fathers as helping them feel special, teachers as helping them stay on track to college, and sisters as helping them with schoolwork, feeling confident, and planning the future. Students making lower math grades were more likely to report providing their own encouragement with math, speaking up for themselves at school, and to name peers as helping with sexism and racism.

Summary

The findings of this study illustrate the continuing significance of adolescents' relationships with family members as well as their teachers, peers, and academic outreach programs. They also underscore the interplay between African American and Latino adolescents' interactions with gatekeepers and brokers as they navigate the academic pipeline from middle and high school to college.

Models of social capital and oppositional identity suggest that students with more capital and fewer structural barriers would achieve at higher levels. Some evidence for these models is reflected in our findings that students with more adult support, as well as educational expertise, were achieving at higher levels. The prediction from the Individuality and Connectedness Model, that challenges in the context of cohesion fosters identity development, is supported by findings that students making higher grades experienced both resources and difficulties, that the same people could be both resources and difficulties, and that difficulties appeared to motivate students to succeed on behalf of their families and to prove gatekeepers wrong. As one Mexican American male high school student wrote: "The most important experience for me did not even happen to me. It happened to my mother. She wanted to go to college and become a professional. She did not accomplish her dream because back then, women were born to be housewives, not professionals. Her parents did not pay for her education because of this." Thus, adolescents' academic identity and self-governance may be fostered by their active engagement in difficulties as a proactive coping strategy and with others in constructing meaning of their experiences (Laosa, 1990; Stanton-Salazar & Dornbusch, 1995). Our finding both resources and difficulties from peers suggests that we should look further into distinguishing experiences that stimulate self-governance from those that undermine it.

In our continuing work with academic outreach programs, we are examining links from ethnically diverse students' relationships and both positive and negative expectations from their worlds to their identity development and academic achievement, including their college attendance. We are particularly interested in students' negotiations with brokers and gatekeepers as they move along the academic pipeline. Based on conceptions of identity development in the context of relationships, we are also tracing how students' views of their resources and challenges reflect their changing views of themselves (Grotevant & Cooper, 1998). Finally, our collaborating academic outreach programs are using the Multiple Worlds Survey for ongoing program analysis in extending their work in urban middle and high schools serving ethnically diverse youth.

CONCLUSIONS AND FUTURE DIRECTIONS

In closing, we emphasize five key points. First, the overarching purpose of the theoretical and empirical work summarized in this chapter has been to understand experiences of *Individuality and Connectedness* in the lives of diverse youth and their relationships across the life span in relation to cultural, institutional, and socioeconomic processes (Cooper, 1994; Grotevant & Cooper, 1998). The conceptual, empirical, and methodological advances reviewed illustrate the continuing value of considering adolescents' constructing a sense of identity as part of the ongoing development of their relationships, institutions, and cultures rather than viewing adolescents either as the only dynamic element in a static culture or as a passive reactor to social, economic, and cultural forces.

Second, the *Ecocultural framework* has been useful in "unpackaging" categorical, global, and static characterizations of diverse groups by identifying dimensions of worlds, including goals and values, personnel, scripts, and activity settings. Ecocultural theory continues to develop in response to empirical work (e.g., Bronfenbrenner, 1988; Gallimore, Goldenberg, & Weisner, 1994; Gallimore, Weisner, Bernheimer, Guthrie, & Nihira, 1993), directing our attention to the ongoing processes of accommodation and adaptation in families.

Phelan, Davidson, and Yu's model of the *Multiple Worlds* of adolescents' families, peers, schools, and communities enriches work based on more static and oppositional "two worlds" models of family versus peers or family versus school. We have learned how adolescents negotiate with others who function as gatekeepers, blocking their way, and brokers, facilitating their way, and that individuals in any world can play either or both roles. By any account, we still have much more to understand about how adolescents navigate through their worlds and confront restrictions such as poverty, violence, and discrimination. The recent work of Phelan's team is illuminating the contributions of ongoing dialogues with adolescents as research collaborators, an approach consistent with our experiences of the value of focus groups throughout research projects (Davidson, 1994, 1996).

Fourth, the *parallel design* proposed by Sue and Sue (1987) challenges us to define developmental constructs or dimensions in culturally specific terms and then map both similarities and differences across cultural communities in their development. We are just beginning to do this with European American and "mainstream" samples, who are often treated in global and stereotypic terms even when other cultural groups are differentiated. In many ways, the most difficult phase of the parallel design involves linking culture-specific, qualitative, and meaning-based or "subjective" data to culturally universal, quantitative, and "objective" data. Because equivalent measures across cultures and languages, despite translations and back-translations, are ideals not always attained in practice, we are devoting more attention to linking qualitative and quantitative approaches (Cooper, Gjerde, Teranishi, & Onishi, 1994; Cooper, Labissière, & Teranishi, 1997; Gaskins, 1994; Matsumoto, 1994; Schofield & Anderson, 1987). The studies described in this chapter illustrate how including open-ended questions in surveys and interviews, with individuals and in groups, helps overcome the inevitable limitations of any one investigator's experiences (Jarrett, 1995).

Finally, beyond any particular theoretical, methodological, or empirical focus, the integrity of research on diversity and development rests on *collaborations among stakeholders*, including children, their families, researchers, and community institutions, and in coordinating the goals, needs, and perspectives of different participants in ways that enhance trust among them (Cooper, Jackson, Azmitia, & Lopez, 1998). Particularly in communities where participants have had tenuous relationships with universities and researchers, such collaborations are ongoing projects reflecting individual, relational, and institutional strengths and vulnerabilities. These collaborations can raise questions not always asked by researchers, such as the appropriate nature of incentives; the risks of disclosing information regarding citizenship, income, occupation, age, ethnicity, generation of immigration, or household membership; and the costs of participation for individuals' and communities' broader goals and loyalties.

This chapter is written in a time of constricting opportunities for education, health, housing, and other services for children, youth, and families in the United States and other nations. Consequently, new coalitions are emerging on behalf of children and families from diverse cultural communities—with businesses, schools, and private and public agencies. The practice of science can function in coordination and collaboration with these individual, relationship, and institutional processes. We have much to contribute and to learn in such partnerships.

ACKNOWLEDGMENTS

The support of National Institute of Child Health and Human Development, the Hogg Foundation for Mental Health, the University Research Institute of the University of Texas at Austin, the Spencer Foundation, the Linguistic Minority Research Institute and the Pacific Rim Foundation of the University of California, the National Center for Research in Cultural Diversity and Second Language Learning of the U.S. Office of Educational Research and Improvement, and the John D. and Catherine T. MacArthur Foundation is gratefully acknowledged. The contributions of collaborators Margarita Azmitia, Harold Grotevant, Per Gjerde, and Jacquelyne Jackson; of my students Edward Lopez, Nora Dunbar, Christy Teranishi, Angela Ittel, and Zena Mello; of colleagues Maureen Callanan, Barbara Rogoff, Vonnie McLoyd, Linda Burton, Cynthia García Coll, Shirley Heath, Richard Shweder, and especially Robert G. Cooper, are appreciated. Finally, the participation and sustained engagement of the youth, families, schools, and academic outreach program staff in the studies described in this chapter are gratefully acknowledged.

REFERENCES

Archer, S. L. (1992). A feminist's approach to identity research. In G. R. Adams, T. P. Gullotta, & R. Montemayor (Eds.), *Advances in adolescent development: Adolescent identity formation* (pp. 25–49). Newbury Park, CA: Sage.

Azmitia, M., & Cooper, C. R. (1997). *Navigating and negotiating home, school, and peer linkages in adolescence.* U.S. Office of Educational Research and Improvement: Center for Research on Education, Diversity, and Excellence.

Azmitia, M., Cooper, C. R., García, E. E., & Dunbar, N. (1996). The ecology of family guidance in low-income Mexican-American and European-American families. *Social Development, 5,* 1–23.

Azmitia, M., Cooper, C. R., García, E. E., Ittel, A., Johanson, B., Lopez, E. M., Martínez-Chávez, R., & Rivera, L. (1994). Links between home and school among low-income Mexican American and European American families. *Educational Practice Report, 9* (pp. 1–28). University of California at Santa Cruz: National Center for Research on Cultural Diversity and Second Language Learning.

Bordieu, P., & Passeron, C. (1977). *Reproduction in education, society and culture.* London: Sage.

Bronfenbrenner, U. (1988). Foreword. In A. R. Pence (Ed.), *Ecological research with children and families: From concepts to methodology* (pp. ix–xix). New York: Teachers College Press.

Carlson, C. I., Cooper, C. R., & Spradling, V. (1991). Developmental implications of shared vs. distinct perceptions of the family in early adolescence. In R. Paikoff (Ed.), *Shared perspectives on the family: New directions for child development, 51* (pp. 13–31). San Francisco: Jossey-Bass.

Cazden, C. B. (1988). *Classroom discourse.* Portsmouth, NH: Heinemann Educational Books.

Chisholm, L., Büchner, P., Krüger, H. H., & Brown, P. (Eds.). (1990). *Childhood, youth, and social change: A comparative perspective.* London: Falmer Press.

Coleman, J. S. (1988). Social capital in the creation of human capital. *American Journal of Sociology Supplement, 94,* 95–120.

Cooper, C. R. (1988). The analysis of conflict in adolescent-parent relationships. In M. R. Gunnar & W. A. Collins (Eds.), *Minnesota Symposium on Child Psychology: Development during the transition to adolescence* (pp. 181–187). Hillsdale, NJ: Lawrence Erlbaum Associates.

Cooper, C. R. (1994). Cultural perspectives on continuity and change in adolescents' relationships. In R. Montemayor, G. R. Adams, & T. P. Gulotta (Eds.), *Advances in adolescent development: Vol. 6. Personal relationships during adolescence* (pp. 78–100). Newbury Park, CA: Sage.

Cooper, C. R., Azmitia, M., García, E. E., Ittel, A., Lopez, E., Rivera, L., & Martínez-Chávez, R. (1994). Aspirations of low-income Mexican American and European American parents for their children and adolescents. In F. Villarruel & R. M. Lerner (Eds.), *Community-based programs for socialization and learning: New directions in child development* (pp. 65–81). San Francisco: Jossey-Bass.

Cooper, C. R., Baker, H., Polichar, D., & Welsh, M. (1993). Values and communication of Chinese, European, Filipino, Mexican, and Vietnamese American adolescents with their families and friends. In S. Shulman & W. A. Collins (Eds.), *Father–adolescent relationships: New directions in child development* (Vol. 62, pp. 73–89). San Francisco: Jossey-Bass.

Cooper, C. R., & Cooper, R. G. (1992). Links between adolescents' relationships with their parents and peers: Models, evidence, and mechanisms. In R. D. Parke & G. W. Ladd (Eds.), *Family-peer relationships: Modes of linkages* (pp. 135–158). Hillsdale, NJ: Lawrence Erlbaum Associates.

Cooper, C. R., & Denner, J. (1998). Theories linking culture and psychology: Universal and community-specific processes. *Annual Review of Psychology, 49,* 559–584.

Cooper, C. R., Gjerde, P. F., Teranishi, C., & Onishi, M. (1994, April). *Antecedents of competence in early and late adolescence: An ecocultural analysis of Japanese, Japanese American, and European American adolescents.* Paper presented at the meeting of the Western Psychological Association, Kona, HI.

Cooper, C. R., Grotevant, H. D., & Condon, S. L. (1983). Individuality and connectedness in the family as a context for adolescent identity formation and role-taking skill. In H. D. Grotevant

& C. R. Cooper (Eds.), *Adolescent development in the family: New directions in child development* (pp. 43–59). San Francisco: Jossey-Bass.

Cooper, C. R., Jackson, J. F., Azmitia, M., Lopez, E. M., & Dunbar, N. (1994). *Multiple selves, multiple worlds survey: Qualitative and quantitative versions.* Santa Cruz: University of California at Santa Cruz.

Cooper, C. R., Jackson, J. F., Azmitia, M., & Lopez, E. M. (1998). Multiple selves, multiple worlds: Ethnically sensitive research on identity, relationships, and opportunity structures in adolescence. In V. McLoyd & L. Steinberg (Eds.), *Conceptual and methodological issues in the study of minority adolescents and their families.* Hillsdale, NJ: Lawrence Erlbaum Associates.

Cooper, C. R., Jackson, J. F., Azmitia, M., Dunbar, N., Lopez, E. M., Cooper, R. G., Figueroa, J., & Cooper, D. C. (1995). *Linking family, school, and peers: African American and Latino youth in university outreach programs.* Paper presented at the meetings of the Society for Research in Child Development, Indianapolis, IN.

Cooper, C. R., Jackson, J. F., Azmitia, M., Lopez, E. M., & Dunbar, N. (1995). Bridging students' multiple worlds: African American and Latino youth in academic outreach programs. In R. F. Macías & R. G. García Ramos (Eds.), *Changing schools for changing students: An anthology of research on language minorities* (pp. 211–234). Santa Barbara: University of California Linguistic Minority Research Institute.

Cooper, C. R., Labissière, Y., & Teranishi, C. (1997). *Strategies for linking qualitative and quantitative analyses of childhood: Lessons from studies of ethnicity and identity.* Final Report to the John D. and Catherine T. MacArthur Foundation Research Network on Successful Pathways Through Childhood.

Davidson, A. L. (1994). Students' situated selves: Ethnographic interviewing as cultural therapy. In G. Spindler & L. Spindler (Eds.), *Pathways to cultural awareness: Cultural therapy with teachers and students* (pp. 131–167). Thousand Oaks, CA: Corwin Press.

Davidson, A. L. (1996). *Making and molding identity in schools: Student narratives on race, gender, and academic engagement.* Albany: State University of New York Press.

Delgado-Gaitan, C. (1993). Research and policy in reconceptualizing family-school relationships. In P. Phelan & A. L. Davidson (Eds.), *Renegotiating cultural diversity in American schools* (pp. 139–159). New York: Teachers College Press.

Eccles, J., Midgley, C., Wigfield, A., Buchanan, C. M., Reuman, D., Flanagan, C., & MacIver, D. (1993). Development during adolescence: The impact of stage-environment fit on young adolescents' experiences in schools and in families. *American Psychologist, 48,* 90–101.

Edgert, P., & Taylor, J. W. (1992). *Final report on the effectiveness of intersegmental student preparation programs: The third report to the Legislature in response to Item 6420-0011-001 of the 1988–89 Budget Act.* Sacramento: California Postsecondary Education Commission.

Erickson, R., & Shultz, J. (1982). *The counselor as gatekeeper: Social interaction in interviews.* New York: Academic Press.

Fordham, S., & Ogbu, J. U. (1986). Black students' school success: Coping with the "burden of 'acting White.' " *The Urban Review, 18,* 176–206.

Gallimore, R., Goldenberg, C. N., & Weisner, T. S. (1993). The social construction and subjective reality of activity settings: Implications for community psychology. *American Journal of Community Psychology, 21,* 537–559.

Gallimore, R., Weisner, T. S., Bernheimer, L. P., Guthrie, D., & Nihira, H. (1993). Family responses to young children with developmental delays: Accommodation activity in ecological and cultural context. *American Journal on Mental Retardation, 98,* 185–206.

Gándara, P., & Osugi, L. (1994). Educationally ambitious Chicanas. *The NEA Higher Education Journal, 10,* 7–35.

García, E. E. (1992). "Hispanic" children: Theoretical, empirical, and related policy issues. *Educational Psychology Review, 4,* 69–93.

Gaskins, S. (1994). Integrating interpretive and quantitative methods in socialization research. *Merrill-Palmer Quarterly, 40,* 313–333.

Goldenberg, C., Reese, L., Balzano, S., & Gallimore, R. (1993, April). *Cause or effect? Latino children's school performance and their parents' educational expectations.* Paper presented at the meetings of the American Educational Research Association, Atlanta, GA.

Goodnow, J. J., & Collins, W. A. (1990). *Development according to parents: The nature, sources, and consequences of parents' ideas.* Hillsdale, NJ: Lawrence Erlbaum Associates.

Greenfield, P. M., & Cocking, R. R. (Eds.). (1994). *Cross-cultural roots of minority child development.* Hillsdale, NJ: Lawrence Erlbaum Associates.

Grotevant, H. D., & Cooper, C. R. (1988). The role of family experience in career exploration during adolescence. In P. B. Baltes, D. L. Featherman, & R. M. Lerner (Eds.), *Life-span development and behavior* (Vol. 8, pp. 231–258). Hillsdale, NJ: Lawrence Erlbaum Associates.

Grotevant, H. D., & Cooper, C. R. (1998). Individuality and connectedness in adolescent development: Review and prospects for research on identity, relationships, and context. In E. Skoe & A. von der Lippe (Eds.), *Personality development in adolescence: A cross national and life span perspective* (pp. 3–37). London: Routledge.

Grotevant, H. D., & Cooper, C. R. (1985). Patterns of interaction in family relationships and the development of identity formation in adolescence. *Child Development, 56,* 415–428.

Grotevant, H. D., & Cooper, C. R. (1986). Individuation in family relationships: A perspective on individual differences in the development of identity and role-taking skill in adolescence. *Human Development, 29,* 82–100.

Haines, D. W. (1988). Kinship in Vietnamese refugee resettlement: A review of the U.S. experience. *Journal of Comparative Family Studies, 19,* 1–16.

Harrison, A. O., Wilson, M. N., Pine, C. J., Chan, S. Q., & Buriel, R. (1990). Family ecologies of ethnic minority children. *Child Development, 61,* 347–362.

Heath, S. B. (1983). *Ways with words: Language, life, and work in communities and classrooms.* New York: Cambridge University Press.

Heath, S. B., & McLaughlin, M. W. (1993). *Identity and inner-city youth: Beyond ethnicity and gender.* New York: Teachers College Press.

Hong, G. K. (1989). Application of cultural and environmental issues in family therapy with immigrant Chinese Americans. *Journal of Strategic and Systematic Therapies, 8,* 14–21.

Jarrett, R. L. (1995). Growing up poor: The family experiences of socially mobile youth in low-income African-American neighborhoods. *Journal of Adolescent Research, 10,* 111–135.

Kroger, J. (1993, April). *The role of historical context in the identify formation process of late adolescence.* Paper presented at the meeting of the Society for Research in Child Development, New Orleans, LA.

Laosa, L. M. (1990). Psychosocial stress, coping, and development of Hispanic immigrant children. In F. C. Serafica, A. I. Schwebel, R. K. Russell, P. D. Isaac, & L. B. Myers (Eds.), *Mental health of ethnic minorities* (pp. 38–65). New York: Praeger.

LeVine, R. A. (1988). Human parental care: Universal goals, cultural strategies, individual behavior. In R. A. LeVine, P. M. Miller, & M. M. West (Eds.), *Parental behavior in diverse societies* (pp. 5–12). San Francisco: Jossey-Bass.

Markus, H. R., & Kitayama, S. (1991). Culture and self: Implications for cognition, emotion, and motivation. *Psychological Review, 98,* 224–253.

Matsumoto, D. (1994). *Cultural influences on research methods and statistics.* Belmont, CA: Brooks/Cole.

McLoyd, V. C. (1991). What is the study of African American children the study of? In R. J. Jones (Ed.), *Black psychology* (pp. 419–440). Berkeley, CA: Cobb & Henry.

McLoyd, V. C., & Flanagan, C. A. (1990). *Economic stress: Effects on family life and child development. New directions for child development.* San Francisco: Jossey-Bass.

Mehan, H., Hubbard, L., Okamoto, D., & Villanueva, I. (1995). Untracking high school students in preparation for college: Implications for Latino students. In A. Hurtado & E. E. García

(Eds.), The educational achievement of Latinos: Barriers and successes (pp. 149–195). Santa Cruz, CA: Regents of the University of California.

Nurmi, J. E., Poole, M. E., & Seginer, R. (1995). Tracks and transitions: A comparison of adolescent future-oriented goals, explorations, and commitments in Australia, Israel and Finland. *International Journal of Psychology, 30,* 355–375.

O'Brien, E. M. (1993). Latinos in higher education. *American Council on Education Research Brief Series, Vol. 4, No. 4.* Washington, DC: American Council on Education.

Ogbu, J. U. (1991). Minority coping responses and school experience. *Journal of Psychohistory, 18,* 433–456.

Parke, R. D., & Ladd, G. W. (Eds.). (1992). *Family-peer relationships: Modes of linkages.* Hillsdale, NJ: Lawrence Erlbaum Associates.

Phelan, P., Davidson, A. L., & Yu, H. C. (1991). Students' multiple worlds: Navigating the borders of family, peer, and school cultures. In P. Phelan & A. L. Davidson (Eds.), *Cultural diversity: Implications for education* (pp. 52–88). New York: Teachers College Press.

Phinney, J. S. (1993). Multiple group identities: Differentiation, conflict, and integration. In J. Kroger (Ed.), *Discussions on ego identity.* Hillsdale, NJ: Lawrence Erlbaum Associates.

Pike, K. L. (1966). *Language in relation to a unified theory of the structure of human behavior.* The Hague, Netherlands: Mouton.

Reese, L., Gallimore, R., Goldenberg, C., & Balzano, C. (1995). Immigrant Latino parents' future orientations for their children. In R. F. Macías & R. G. García Ramos (Eds.), *Changing schools for changing students: An anthology of research on language minorities.* Santa Barbara: University of California Linguistic Minority Research Institute.

Rodman, H., & Voydanoff, P. (1988). Social class and parents' range of aspirations for their children. *Journal of Social Issues, 23,* 333–344.

Rogoff, B. (1990). *Apprenticeship in thinking: Cognitive development in social context.* New York: Oxford University Press.

Sabogal, F., Marín, G., Otero-Sabogal, R., VanOss Marín, B. V., & Perez-Stable, E. J. (1987). Hispanic familism and acculturation: What changes and what doesn't? *Hispanic Journal of Behavioral Sciences, 9,* 397–412.

Santos, R. A. (1983). The social and emotional development of Filipino-American children. In G. J. Powell, J. Yamamoto, A. Romero, & A. Morales (Eds.), *The psychosocial development of minority group children.* New York: Brunner/Mazel.

Schofield, J. W., & Anderson, K. (1987). Combining quantitative and qualitative components of research on ethnic identity and intergroup relations. In J. S. Phinney & M. J. Rotheram (Eds.), *Childrens' ethnic socialization: Pluralism and development.* Newbury Park, CA: Sage.

Skolnick, A. (1993). Changes of heart: Family dynamics in historical perspective. In P. A. Cowan, D. Field, D. A. Hansen, A. Skolnick, & G. E. Swanson (Eds.), *Family, self, and society: Toward a new agenda for family research* (pp. 43–68). Hillsdale, NJ: Lawrence Erlbaum Associates.

Smetana, J. G. (1988). Concepts of self and social convention: Adolescents' and parents' reasoning about hypothetical and actual family conflicts. In M. R. Gunnar & W. A. Collins (Eds.), *Transitions to adolescence: 21st Minnesota Symposism on Child Psychology* (pp. 79–122). Hillsdale, NJ: Lawrence Erlbaum Associates.

Spencer, M. B., & Dornbusch, S. M. (1990). Challenges in studying minority youth. In S. S. Feldman & G. R. Eliot (Eds.), *At the threshold: The developing adolescent* (pp. 123–146). Cambridge, MA: Harvard University Press.

Stanton-Salazar, R. D., & Dornbusch, S. M. (1995). Social capital and the social reproduction of inequality: Information networks among Mexican-origin high school students. *Sociology of Education, 68,* 116–135.

Steward, E. W., & Shamdasani, P. N. (1990). *Focus groups: Theory and practice.* Newbury Park, CA: Sage.

Suarez-Orozco, M. M. (1991). Immigrant adaptation to schooling: A Hispanic case. In M. A. Gibson & J. U. Ogbu (Eds.), *Minority status and schooling* (pp. 37–162). New York: Garland.

Sue, D., & Sue, S. (1987). Cultural factors in the clinical assessment of Asian Americans. *Journal of Consulting and Clinical Psychology, 55*, 479–487.

Takanishi, R. (1994). Continuities and discontinuities in the cognitive socialization of Asian-originated children: The case of Japanese Americans. In P. M. Greenfield & R. R. Cocking (Eds.), *Cross-cultural roots of minority child development.* Hillsdale, NJ: Lawrence Erlbaum Associates.

Tharp, R. G., & Gallimore, R. (1988). *Rousing minds to life: Teaching learning and schooling in social context.* Cambridge, England: Cambridge University Press.

Tienda, M. (1980). Familism and structural assimilation of Mexican immigrants in the United States. *International Migration Review, 14*, 383–408.

Triandis, H. C. (1995). *Individualism and collectivism.* Boulder, CO: Westview Press.

Trueba, H. T. (1991). Linkages of macro-micro analytical levels. *The Journal of Psychohistory, 18*, 457–468.

Weisner, T. S., Gallimore, R., & Jordan, C. (1988). Unpacking cultural effects on classroom learning: Native Hawaiian peer assistance and child-generated activity. *Anthropology and Education Quarterly, 19*, 327–351.

Whiting, B. (1976). The problem of the packaged variable. In K. Riegal & J. Meacham (Eds.), *The developing individual in a changing world: Historical and cultural issues: Vol. 1* (pp. 303–309). The Hague, Netherlands: Mouton.

Yao, J., & Smetana, J. G. (1993). Chinese American adolescents' reasoning about cultural conflicts. *Journal of Adolescent Research, 8*, 419–438.

Youniss, J., & Smollar, J. (1985). *Adolescent relations with mothers, fathers, and friends.* Chicago: University of Chicago Press.

Chapter 3

Dimensions of Language Development: Lessons From Older Children

Shirley Brice Heath
Stanford University

Development of language goes on throughout life. Language learning is truly lifelong. Speakers continue to acquire morphemes to build vocabulary, stylistic variation in syntax, and pragmatic maneuvers to meet needs that shift according to interlocutors, acquired bodies of knowledge, and altered roles. Investigators of first language development have given almost no attention to how such learning takes place, what may motivate it, and the speed with which vocabulary growth and syntactic complexity can take place beyond early childhood (but see Hoyle & Adger, 1998). The focus of this chapter is the language development of older children and young people over a relatively brief time frame within project-based environments of intense peer interaction guided by one or more adults. Situations for this learning occur within out-of-school youth-based organizations that involve young members primarily in either the arts and service or athletics with a strong focus on academics.

To begin, I briefly review the history of child language studies since the 1960s. I then address the nature of research on the language development of older children and argue that the kind of heuristic that guides contemporary theorizing about language development does not speak to the reality of later continuing language learning. I illustrate with data from a multiyear study of language uses among peers within youth-based organizations.

STUDIES IN CHILD LANGUAGE

Child language researchers have centered their research on language development almost exclusively on infants and toddlers and on environments that include only mother and child. Only one major overview of language acquisition (Romaine, 1984) addresses adolescents and their competence in language; two substantial investigations (Eckert, 1989; Goodwin, 1990) detail language patterns of older children within a repertoire of styles and uses. Eckert (1989) illustrates how sound change spreads through age cohorts of high school students as they identify as either "jocks" or "burnouts." Goodwin (1990) describes ways in which males and females in an African American urban environment use talk to structure the worlds of their daily social interactions. Occasional articles on one or another routine in the speech of older children appear; for example, Gleason and Weintraub (1976) detail how children from just under 6 to about 12 acquire the "trick or treat" routine.

The *Journal of Child Language* has since its initial issue in 1974 included reports of research primarily concerned with children before they enter school. Most such studies have taken place in either laboratories or homes where the leisure of the mother allows scheduling of regular visits by researchers. In both cases, those who collect data carry strong assumptions of the prevalence of stable nuclear families with mothers who do not work outside the home who can follow regular schedules and devote a major portion of their attention to their firstborn child. This is a situation fast disappearing in complex societies where children spend most of their weekday hours in group childcare facilities from the time of their birth until they enter school.

However, strong expectations of extended sessions between mother and child in isolation continue to dominate early language studies. This work follows models of research established in the late 1960s when psychologists and linguists, primarily from Berkeley, Harvard, and Stanford, came together to compare and refine "modern techniques of study to children" (Slobin, 1967, p. viii). Collected papers and bibliographies of theory and research on child language (e.g., Abrahamsen, 1977; Bar-Adon & Leopold, 1971; Ferguson & Slobin, 1973; Gleason, 1985; Slobin, 1985a, 1985b; Snow & Ferguson, 1977) over the next two decades continued a primary focus on investigations of the acquisition of morphology or syntax by firstborn children in mother–child interactions within the first years of the child's life within the family at home or with the mother in laboratory tasks. Jakobson's (1941) early work on the acquisition of phonology found no followings until the foundation of the Child Phonology Project at Stanford University in the 1970s (Ferguson, Menn, & Stoel-Gammon, 1992), and few investigators outside this group put phonology on a par with morphology and syntax in their research. Notable exceptions to the interactional frame of mother and child were studies of monologic talk by children alone in their crib replaying portions of language they heard about them often during the same or prior day (Kuczaj, 1983; Nelson, 1989; Weir, 1970).

Initial studies taking into account language development of older children centered primarily on their acquisition of school-approved forms and uses in contrast to their at-home talk, their growth of metalinguistic awareness, or their within-group routines of dispute, teasing, and friendship bonding (Cazden, 1972; Cazden, John, & Hymes, 1971; Ervin-Tripp & Mitchell-Kernan, 1977). Beginning in the late 1960s, with the work of William Labov and associates on "nonstandard English" within peer groups (Labov, 1972; Labov, Cohen, & Robins, 1965; Labov, Cohen, Robins, & Lewis, 1968), sociolinguists branched out from the acquisitional interests of child language researchers to give almost exclusive attention to language variation and social interactions. Much of this work characterized the complex and rule-ordered nature of particular discourse forms, such as narratives and "dozens," and their work of challenge and aggression within peer groups of adolescent males outside the home and school (Abrahams, 1964; Labov & Waletzky, 1967). Little or no attention has gone to how young speakers absorb into their ordinary conversation specific morphemes, increasingly complex syntactic structures, semantic webs, or particular registers and genres.

THE TALK OF OLDER CHILDREN AND LEARNERS

Once children enter school, their language becomes the target of teachers and speech therapists who look at their talk in terms of appropriateness and match to normal development patterns. Hence the major portion of investigations of language for school-age children centers either on language disorders or the acquisition of particular ways of responding to adults (specifically teacher talk) or props presented by adults (such as books, worksheets, and so forth). Psychologists also give considerable attention to the understanding of prepositions and temporal adverbs by early school-age children in an attempt to understand their grasp of spatial and temporal relations.

Much of the research on children of the elementary grades has then centered not on their productive abilities as speakers (a notable exception is Loban, 1963), but on either their writing abilities or their interpretive skills, as well as the role of interactional processes within the specific situation of the classroom and of the testing situations there (Cicourel, 1974; Heath, 1978; Mehan, 1979). The social nature of language use, as well as the constructed culture- and situation-specific norms of appropriateness came to be a major focus of such work by the early 1980s, but this emphasis emerged only very gradually out of growing recognition of the influence of culture on human development.

Anthropologists of education had since the 1960s carried out comparative studies of home socialization patterns and their conflicts with expectations of classroom usage and assessment performances (e.g., Spindler, 1963; Wax, Wax, & Dumont, 1964). But language practices received relatively little attention within socialization until the 1980s, when the importance of language as instrument and focus of enculturation and particularly of communicative strategies for adaptation to mainstream institutional demands drew the attention of investigators. Socialization through language and socialization to use language emerged in a comparative frame, demonstrating the different expectations held across institutions of socialization, ranging from family to school to workplace to particular professional and informal groupings. Investigators have especially focused their studies on the difficulties for young children that these various norms and processes across social interactional settings hold, as well as the contrasts across different cultural groups of early socialization patterns (Heath, 1983; Schieffelin & Ochs, 1986a, 1986b).

Although acknowledging the need to understand how older children and adults adjust to new language learning demands, scholars have rarely moved up the age spectrum of older children to examine what happens as their language develops across social interactions, roles, and institutional memberships. Almost every study of language learning demands in the mother tongue for adult speakers is a single case: for example, learning to think and talk like a physician, police officer, sports enthusiast, or wine connoisseur (Drew & Heritage, 1992; Ferguson, 1983; Lehrer, 1983; McElhinny, 1993). Almost all this work has been done by sociologists and sociolinguists. None of these studies is acquisitional, but each shows language skills necessary to belong to a particular leisure activity circle or professional community; implicit is the role of language socialization behind such membership. *The Journal of Adult Learning*, drawing primarily psychologists as authors, rarely includes studies of how adults become socialized to and through the language of new situations and roles.

The few studies that attend to older children and young adults learning language on-the-job or within new avocations illustrate the interdependence of affect and motivation with sense of community and role. In an ethnography of one community-based organization dependent for its funding on grants and positive perceptions by the local political and civic community, Beaufort (1995) demonstrated the organization's increasingly complex situations for learning specialized genres and styles of writing very rapidly: "writing was a shared responsibility of the community, with some members taking leadership roles as writers and others taking lesser writing roles" (p. 85). But these responsibilities and roles shifted almost from day to day as new demands appeared; as many as 15 distinct writing roles could be assumed by any of the middle-level management employees of the agency. This study and others of adults new to tasks and institutional roles point out that while learning new ways of talking and writing, individuals take on group membership, decide on roles that suit their talents, develop strategies for fast learning curves, and manipulate themselves into apprentice-like circumstances so as to observe and participate as they learn (Lave & Wenger, 1991).

Theories of learning that have developed around this work repeatedly demonstrate the embeddedness of language within activities and the legitimation that using language offers individuals as group members. Task orientation and overall structural organization and role possibilities thus shape language use to a great extent, although speakers and writers can usually choose, though often for only a limited period of time and for only specific components and stages of tasks, the roles they wish to play. They may, for example, in some learning situations, where they do not know the vocabulary or way of talking about the task at hand, select a quiet observing role, or they may select one or more individuals as mentor for demonstration or explication. Neutral stances rarely offer themselves as options, because of either or both task/activity and legitimation of individual within group, and often, of the group itself with respect to accomplishment of the task. Just as young children, with practice and attachment to certain interactional goals, learn routines of language, so older children and adults develop standard practices for managing and negotiating encounters, collaborative opportunities, and task assignments within activities. Opportunities to practice both oral and written language lead to automaticity in the use of routines as well as enable the build-up of a series of strategies for learning language and repairing mistakes. Often these strategies include practicing silently, as well as seeking in isolation written textual forms that one is expected to learn to handle orally. Current professionals, especially academics raised within families and communities that offered little in the way of intellectual discourse, sometimes confess that as older children they developed highly elaborate ways to avoid having their deficiencies in academic language socialization detected (Rose, 1989).

The usual type of heuristic that guides contemporary theorizing about language development of very young children remains insufficiently social or metalinguistic to address these realities of language development. When we conceive of development as "transformation of participation" through membership in a community of learners (Rogoff, 1994), we are forced to attend to how activity and roles shape language learning. Individuals gain access to legitimation as group members, while also working to help the group legitimate itself through the shared sociocultural endeavors that result in some outcome or goal achievement. The stakes are high for acceptable social membership for such individuals and the punishments immediate and often unrelenting from peers, bosses, and teachers; thus legitimation by (and through) language can be vital, and speed of acquisition may become critical. The nurturing, patient, predictable environment of mother–child interaction and the absence of task and rigid role expectations offer no such tensions and may mask many of the contextual and affective factors behind the language learning of older speakers. Culture, context, intense stress, improbabilities of membership and belonging, as well as embeddedness within task, do not figure in the usual guides for the study of early language development, though they may be essential in accounting for verbal learning of older children and adults.

We turn now to an examination of material gathered among older children engaged as group members within specific tasks over an extended period of time within organizations for youth where such tensions center on the activities and legitimation demands of the group. These data illustrate for theory construction the multiple factors that work interdependently to motivate changes in linguistic practices of the young speakers.

LEARNING AT WORK "TO PROVE" SOMETHING

In the final decades of the 20th century when work seems to be increasingly important to adults, opportunities for young people to engage in work have greatly decreased. Here the distinction between *work* and *jobs* is critical. Someone else provides *jobs* as well as assessment of how well or how poorly one does them. But *work* of the sort implied in statements such as "I've got to work on cleaning the garage (or refinishing my dad's boat, etc.)" involves preparing, planning, executing, and assessing tasks for oneself and within a larger whole than the specific task at hand. A large portion of American adults garner meaning and purpose from work and increasingly substitute organizational structures linked to work for family structures.

Yet for today's young, work within families and neighborhoods with an adult or older peer has almost entirely disappeared. Household chores may be available, but sustained involvement between parent and child in a work project that extends over a period of time occurs rarely. Even middle-class youngsters report that their most sustained time of interaction with parents comes in the family car during vacation travel (Csikszentmihalyi & Larson, 1984). The absence of work between old and young in families and communities means a changed linguistic environment and patterns of language socialization that differ greatly from those typically assumed in the child language literature.

Without extensive and repeated opportunities for work in an apprentice-like role, the young receive little practice in use of linguistic forms that represent planning, cause-and-effect linkages, and scope-and-sequence layouts of what is to come ahead. Joint work, especially between an adult and child or young person, brings with it talk of the sort "what if we, . . ." or "if we do x, then. . . ." Hypothetical constructions involving counterfactual conditionals come embedded in communication around joint work tasks. Similarly, mental state verbs, such as *believe, think,* and so forth, also come with joint tasks, in which one party asks another for opinions or for solutions to stumbling blocks in tasks. Conjoined discourse around achievement of work brings with it ways of thinking and of scripting possible actions and outcomes that few other interactions bring. As single-parent households and families with both parents working outside the home make up over 90% of the population, such opportunities fall primarily to peer interactions.

However, constructive joint work for peers almost never develops without adult supervision. Well-known, however, are forms of illegitimate and covert work orchestrated in youth affiliations or gangs, arranged hierarchically along a corporate structure model. Ironically, within these groups, joint work with older and younger bound together in common pursuits comes to substitute for the expert–novice associations unavailable in both families and schools.

Journalists and politicians blame membership in such groups on "an identity crisis," "peer pressure," and "rebellion and resistance" and heavily pathologize young people who move together as a group in public places (Griffin, 1993; Males, 1996). In the mid-1990s, media campaigns often refer to the young as "predators," "wolfpacks," and "killer kids," while ignoring the writings of economists, sociologists, and criminologists that point out the high levels of violence *against* children and youth (Ehrenreich, 1996). In 1994, the social well-being of the nation reached its lowest point in 25 years; for the first time since 1979, four of the six children and youth indicators—child abuse, teen-age suicide, drug abuse, and high school dropout rate—worsened (Miringoff, 1996). But persistent still are images of "Generation X" as pleasure-seeking and nonempathetic, if not socially irresponsible and violent (Cohen & Krugman, 1994). All of these accusations come without careful consideration of the drastically diminished adult–older child work environments. Many of the qualities and forms of expression that today's young people are said to lack come primarily through long-term engagement with older models around work meaningful to both.

This chapter draws from research carried out between 1987 and 1997 in positive work and learning environments that young people found for themselves in their communities. Considered here is evidence from organizations that regard youth not as problems in need of solutions, but as resources for their communities, families, and each other. This study includes youngsters between the ages of 8 and 18 in urban and rural neighborhoods, as well as in mid-sized cities (25,000–100,000) who are, for one reason or another, separated for the majority of their time from academic role models and stable nuclear family structures. The youth spend up to 40% of their time with one another in cross-age groups working with an adult in projects related to art, service, or athletics and academics. The youth have come voluntarily to join organizations they regard as effective in their lives, as places they want to be to work as a member of a group directed toward a common goal.

These organizations include local affiliates of national organizations, such as Boys and Girls Clubs, Girls, Inc., or Girl Scouts, as well as grassroots dance and theatre groups, or athletic teams that require extensive academic work in the after-school hours. The young people who come to these organizations see themselves "marginalized" in their schools and feared by adults of mainstream institutions and often by adults of their own residential neighborhoods as well. Males and females tend to operate for the most part in separate and different worlds, with many of their encounters with adults in institutions such as school taking place when a group of young people face one or two adults, often under circumstances characterized by conflict.

Data for this chapter come from a multiyear study of the microinteractions of young people in voluntary organizations they join seeking activities and friends in safe environments (Heath, 1995; Heath & McLaughlin, 1994). All organizations studied were located in communities with low funding levels for schools, few recreational resources for youth, high rates of family distress, and disturbing evidence of psychosocial trauma in the lives of children and youth. In the groups they form within these organizations, young people work together with an adult over an extended period of time to bring about the successful performance or completion of some project or activity that depends on individual and group skill and knowledge building. Arts, service, athletics, and educational projects characterize the work of these organizations, led by adults who bring young people into roles of responsibility and direction within the organization. Older youth teach younger members, and for those who remain over several years in the group, they gradually take on roles ranging from receptionist or counsellor to publicist and custodian. Running through most of these organizations is a strong ethos of learning-to-learn in order to maintain themselves within school and to prepare for work outside of school. The organizations see themselves largely in paradoxical relationships with schools; although adult leaders want youth to stay in school and do well there, they also view schools as places that "tear down learning" and disconnect young people from meaningful motivations for learning.

Projects within the youth organizations always run through a full cycle from planning and preparation through practice to performance and evaluation by an external audience. Whether the county art show, final drama performance, or playoffs in basketball or baseball, the final accounting of success for the group and individual performance comes from sources outside the youth organization.

The language used by youth and adult leaders was recorded (in selected organizations representing the 120 youth groups involving 30,000 youngsters studied over a decade) during all phases of the cycle of activities toward completion of the project or final performance. These audiorecordings were transcribed and examined through a combined process of statistical analysis and discourse analysis. The former indicated frequency of particular items (such as modal verbs, negatives, *if–then* constructions) in coordination with turn-taking between adults and young people and in co-occurrence with number of weeks of involvement in the project. Close analysis of the textual materials allowed identification of particular genres (narratives, jokes, strings of directives), and coordination of language data with fieldnotes set this analysis within the context of ongoing nonverbal activities (such as fly-ball practice, writing of dramatic scripts, setup for refreshments for visitors).

Taperecordings that the young people made themselves while no adults were present permitted spot check comparisons between the language used with and in response to adult leaders and that used in tasks when such leaders were not present. For example, adult leaders within a Boys and Girls Club's drama program guide practice and script writing, as well as improvisation exercises and task assignments. However, when the troupe travels for regional youth conventions or drama festivals, young people stay in motel rooms in groups, and their discussions of their own and other groups' performances take place without adults. Junior ethnographers from among the young people, carefully trained in the ethics and methods of taperecording and transcribing, audiorecorded such occasions and provided tape, transcription, and interpretive feedback during review of the transcripts with a senior researcher.

During the planning and preparation phases of all types of youth activities that require "coaching" or "directing" (see Heath & Langman, 1994), adults increasingly engage the young people in hypothetical situations and invite them through sociodramatic bids or "let's pretend" situations. If the group convenes more than three times a week during the initial stages of their project, the percentage of utterances (over 10 morphemes in length) that include either conditionals (if–then constructions), what-if questions, or sociodramatic bids reaches 82%. These utterances establish *irrealis* conditions that insert "real" performance or game conditions within the current planning or practice session. For example, the director asks, "what if we take that scene and shorten it but tie it onto the beginning of what is now scene three? what will the timing look like?" Similarly, the baseball coach may set up a "real" situation by announcing during a practice session focusing on catching: "Top of the seventh inning, Riley's on first, Jason on third, score's tied; Ramsey hits a fly to left field" [coach then hits a fly to left field and discussion follows of what actually happens as players catch it and make decisions about where to throw the ball].

The youth respond initially by observing but give no answers. But sometime within the first six sessions, over 50% of the youngsters respond in some way, either verbally or nonverbally within a few seconds after the query. Within 2 weeks, if meetings occur as often as three times a week, young people toss back their own hypothetical situations. As the project moves from planning and preparation to practice, the young people increase the percentage of conditionals, what-if questions, and sociodramatic bids in their own language, both within adult-led activities and in their peer-only talk. Depending on the length of the course of the project's cycle from beginning to end, newcomers or first-timers within the youth organization increase the percentage of such utterances from less than 2% to more than 62% between opening and closing week.

At the outset of the seasonal cycle, adults take up on the average 84 of every 100 turns, whereas at the peak of the practice period, adult turns drop to about 35 and youth share the remainder of the turns. Generalizing across all types of activity groups within youth organizations, we find that during this peak period for youth talk, about 80% of their utterances of more than 10 words will be hypotheticals or sociodramatic bids. During the evaluation period of the season cycle, this figure reaches about 30%, about the same percentage as definitive statements during this period.

For the youth, their language participation shifts gradually from situations in which they hear and see demonstrated certain syntactic and discourse forms to those in which they must use these forms orally. Here they must build their vocabulary and repertoire of knowledge about types and names of mainstream institutions and increase their written competence with these forms. Adults begin during the planning and preparation phases by illustrating many hypothetical forms using conditional and sociodramatic plays. But they then establish tasks and role-playing situations in which older members of the group guide others. Transcriptions of youth coaches (who had been with the team for 3 years and then asked to take over practice with younger members of an athletic group) show parallels in patterns of language use with those of adult coaches. In taking on the role of coach, younger counterparts also take up the talk. Although less obvious as a role, the same pattern emerges as individual young people take on more and more decision-making roles within the organizations: They learn to speak like someone who knows how to plan, implement, and assess decisions.

Over the course of the activities of the projects and the passage of at least 6 weeks of meetings three times a week or more, over 84% of the individual team members increased their rate of involvement in oral language exchanges. A substantial shift in type of linguistic contribution also occurred. Questions at the outset centered on management and rules: For example, "What happens if we're late?" Once the activity was underway in sustained practice, talk centered on process and possibilities. The following transcript, drawn from the third week of practice of a team preparing to coach participants in track and field events of a Special Olympics, illustrates this type of talk. The novices are not yet present, so the team members take up different roles as they practice their coaching.

JR: [demonstrating to others of the group] as you approach the bar, strong leg goes up first, your back arches, your chin touches down to you [unintelligible], not as low as it goes, just down. Your head goes over, and you kind of arch your back and when your legs are, almost this far, you kick 'em, and you should come down on your back. Alright?

SR: [referring to the two different types of high jump techniques] which one is easier?

JR: uh, for me, for me the 'flop' is easier. Some people might prefer the straddle.

Leader: what's the 'J' approach? [pause] Like the letter 'J'?

JR: ya. Want me to show you?

JI: [to Leader] five steps for the 'J' approach?

JR: no, do you want me to show you?

Leader: Ya.

JR: alright [to Leader] you wanna show 'em? wait, wait, wait. I'll show 'em the 'flop,' you show 'em the straddle. [demonstration continues]

Illustrated in this transcript is the extent to which activity scripts the language of the two speakers. Noticeable here also is the assumption of coaching role young team members take toward their coach, as they offer to show him particular types of high-jump techniques. The ongoing nature of the activity and analytical stance taken by participants here ensures sustained language on topic within a discourse form that stresses constant comparison and awareness of components and scope-and-sequence of a process.

Among themselves, in the spot recordings done by the youth when no adult was present, uses of structures that mark planful behavior or creation of hypothetical future scenarios around a key incident or problem increased from 2 per 100 utterance exchanges (switches from one speaker to another) to 8 per 100. More important than this increase, however, is the display of persistence in following through implications of early posings of "what if?" with several moves or the consideration of several variables. The following exchange that takes place as two girls discuss summer jobs on the way to practice illustrates this point.

D: I have three jobs

N: Do you? I was going to get you a job at the housing authorities

D: huh. How much can I make?

N: four twenty-five an hour

D: where at? Doing what though?

N: clerical, typing, filing

D: I'll still think about it [pause] cuz then [if I get the job you mention]
      I could have four jobs, I could just work McDonald's on the weekends
      and just forget about a Saturday off

N: who needs Saturday off, right?

D: that's right. Who needs a day off?

N: ya

D: no, but that, that's probably like in the mornings, right?

N: [if I do this, then] my schedule gon' get real busy, watch. Cuz [if I take
      on all these jobs, then] I'll be working [pause] overtime still [pause]
      going to school. So [if I do all this, then] I [will] have to schedule to
      go to school on the days I don't work over time. [If I do all this, then]
      I can't, I don't foresee me taking a vacation 'til . . . Christmas.

This conversation between two young women shows four returns to future
scenario-building—a language skill and discourse feature necessary for
both problem-identification and solution. Conversation among peers in
the early weeks of engagement in youth organizations reflects rapid change
of topic, few sustained cases of turn-taking on a single topic, and almost
no multiple linguistic moves of conjecture around future events.

Within the organizational activities, it is possible also to document increased writing, changes in attitudes to writing, and confidence in taking
up new discourse challenges, such as requesting travel information from
an airline agent over the telephone. The shifting roles and demands of
specific tasks provide widening arenas of practice for the youth as they
move into more roles that give them responsibilities within and for the
group as a whole. Also changing over the course of the seasonal cycle are
sources of information called upon in the talk by youth. At the outset of
the season, they draw on personal experience and preface many of their
points with "I." As the season moves forward, they increase their references
to sources outside their own experience as well as to verifiable sources
(such as written texts, videos, and other references that are retrievable).
They also become more comfortable with the array of tasks they have to
assume for the organizations: calling to arrange travel for the group, to
check on insurance costs, to reschedule van pickups, and so on. They have
to do these jobs well; reputation and legitimation of the group depend
on their reflecting well on their peers.

One goal of adult leaders within these organizations is to enable youth
to be self-conscious in their use of language, reflective and self-critical

about what their discourse does and does not accomplish, and gradually comfortable and habituated in their language forms. Rather than learned helplessness in language, the youth take on a learned helpfulness approach to oral and written language and to the types of information, argumentation, and presentation that accomplish work.

CONCLUSIONS

Language development of older children and young adults in a wide variety of sociocultural and institutional settings merits much more attention than linguists and other social scientists, such as psychologists and anthropologists, interested in development have given it. Such work will move investigators away from taking as given circumstances and settings that naturally vary across cultures, situations, and groupings of different ages. Around the world, sociopolitical circumstances have forced separations of the young from adults in a host of ways. For example, since the late 1970s in South African townships, when the young led the protests that sparked the beginning of the end of apartheid, young people have developed a language spoken primarily by young males. Rejecting the "ethnic" groupings that apartheid governments tried to carve out, young people in townships, especially those around Johannesburg, subvert traditional ethnic identifications and clear separations of groups by language spoken. Consequently, children from a very young age learn not only the language of their parents and adult neighbors, but also Iscamtho, the urban *lingua franca* spoken almost exclusively by township males with a base of Sotho and Zulu (Ntshangase, 1995). This language also has a complex sign language (Brookes, in press). Illustrating similar complex patterns of language development and multilingualism are young people in Great Britain who learn enough of one another's language to talk about their common interests (industrial music, chess, sports), even when these languages carry low prestige in the larger society (Rampton, 1995).

Studies embracing a far broader range of settings and connections will surely underscore the situatedness of language learning and its ties to activity. These ties come most often through roles and stances that speakers take up as group members (cf. Rogoff, 1994). For example, there is no pattern in the studies of development of language among older children to suggest that simply being able to produce a particular linguistic construction ties into the context or role in which such constructions may be in high demand. Thus even though no one would doubt that every neurologically normal English-speaking 5-year-old can produce *if–then* constructions, it is a far step from such productions to sustained hypothetical

reasoning within problem solving in an activity. We know that school materials for 10-year-olds in most complex societies begin to call far more
frequently than textbooks of earlier years for building imaginary scenarios
and reasoning out problems. Invariably, it is at this point in their academic
career that many youngsters begin to fall behind. These are the very young
people who never enter high-level science and mathematics classes during
high school and remain in basic classes that call for relatively little extended
discourse around activities that engage learners in responsible role taking.

In the study reported here, I argue that a full understanding of language
development and its role in learning is inextricably entangled with activity
and legitimation of self as a group member and of the activities of the
group (Heath & McLaughlin, 1993). Peer learning, as well as the taking
on of particular roles that have certain language demands, provides opportunities for close investigation of change over a period of time required
for a given activity. Many features of such language learning are principled
and certainly neither so random nor complex as to defy detection. Moreover, it seems clear that particular kinds of youth organizations and adult
shaping of the life of these groups offer certain predictable kinds of arenas
for specific syntactic and discourse forms. When an organization's adults
view young members as part of the group and as vital to accomplishment
of the group's *work*, young learners become embedded in ever widening
frames for building future scenarios—from the task at hand to the particular scene or act of a drama or inning of a ball game to future outcomes.
Language development follows from activity and roles that legitimate membership and overarching purpose of the group.

In more general terms, it is useful to pause and consider the number
of times a task is assigned to an older child or adult, and the immediate
question is "But what do I say?" For example, if an older child is asked to
go next door and borrow the neighbor's folding chairs, the child will often
respond by asking for the words to say. Adults advised to offer condolences,
tone down a fellow worker's anger, or lure the recipient of a surprise
birthday party away for the afternoon will frequently respond by asking
"what should I say?" These instances represent one the few cases in which
specific word and phrase coaching takes place for older speakers. Yet new
forms and uses of language far more complex than these examples are
learned constantly as individuals become socialized through and to uses
of language in particular groups they enter as they mature. Language is
clearly a major force in the continuing socialization of individuals as group
members.

In acquiring language, children—younger and older, as well as adults,
acquire the social systems that embed language. In particular, the learning
of certain registers (e.g., of salesperson, "responsible teenager"), routines
(openings and closings of interviews), and genres (autobiographies that

hit the right balance between self-promotion and humility) can determine in large part acceptance and continuity within groups whose membership may be vital. The psychological and linguistic strategies and impacts of later language learning certainly merit attention.

In brief and in specific terms, I argue here that there are regularities in youth groups that make it possible to study the learning of specific forms and discourse types of language there. Thus development and adaptation of linguistic constructions deemed critical to particular behaviors (e.g., planning) present themselves as highly appropriate for improving our understanding of complex problem solving and adaptation in learning.

ACKNOWLEDGMENT

This research was funded by a grant to Heath and Milbrey W. McLaughlin, School of Education, Stanford University, from the Spencer Foundation.

REFERENCES

Abrahams, R. (1964). *Deep down in the jungle: Negro narrative folklore from the streets of Philadelphia.* Chicago: Aldine.

Abrahamsen, A. A. (1977). *Child language: An interdisciplinary guide to theory and research.* Baltimore: University Park Press.

Bar-Adon, A., & Leopold, W. (Eds.). (1971). *Child language: A book of readings.* Englewood Cliffs, NJ: Prentice-Hall.

Beaufort, A. (1995). *Writing the organization's way: The life of writers in the workplace.* Unpublished dissertation, Stanford University.

Brookes, H. (in press). Sign language in Iscamtho. *Journal of Linguistic Anthropology.*

Cazden, C. B. (1972). *Child language and education.* New York: Holt, Rinehart & Winston.

Cazden, C. B., John, V., & Hymes, D. (Eds.). (1971). *The functions of language in the classroom.* New York: Teachers College Press.

Cicourel, A. V. (1974). Some basic theoretical issues in the assessment of the child's performance in testing and classroom settings. In A. V. Cicourel et al. (Eds.), *Language use and school performance* (pp. 300–365). New York: Academic Press.

Cohen, J., & Krugman, M. (1994). *Generation Ecch!: The backlash starts here.* New York: Simon & Schuster.

Csikszentmihalyi, M., & Larson, R. (1984). *Being adolescent: Conflict and growth in the teenage years.* New York: Basic Books.

Drew, P., & Heritage, J. (Eds.). (1992). *Talk at work: Interaction in institutional settings.* Cambridge, England: Cambridge University Press.

Eckert, P. (1989). *Jocks and jells: Social identity in the high school.* New York: Teachers College Press.

Ehrenreich, B. (1996). Oh, grow up! *Time,* November 4, 1996, p. 100.

Ervin-Tripp, S., & Mitchell-Kernan, C. (1977). *Child discourse.* New York: Academic Press.

Ferguson, C. A. (1983). Sports announcer talk: Syntactic aspects of register variation. *Language in Society, 12,* 153–172.

Ferguson, C. A., Menn, L., & Stoel-Gammon, C. (Eds.). (1992). *Phonological development: Models, research, implications.* Timonium, MD: York Press.

Ferguson, C. A., & Slobin, D. I. (Eds.). (1973). *Studies of child language development.* New York: Holt, Rinehart & Winston.

Gleason, J. B. (1985). *The development of language.* Columbus, OH: Charles E. Merrill.

Gleason, J. B., & Weintraub, S. (1976). The acquisition of routines in child language. *Language in Society, 5,* 129–136.

Goodwin, M. H. (1990). *He-said-she-said: Talk as social organization among black children.* Bloomington: Indiana University Press.

Griffin, C. (1993). *Representations of youth: The study of youth and adolescence in Britain and America.* Cambridge, England: Polity Press.

Heath, S. B. (1978). *Teacher talk: Language in the classroom.* Arlington, VA: Center for Applied Linguistics/ERIC Clearinghouse on Languages and Linguistics, Language in Education Series 9.

Heath, S. B. (1983). *Ways with words: Language, life, and work in communities and classrooms.* New York: Cambridge University Press.

Heath, S. B. (1995). Race, ethnicity and the defiance of categories. In W. E. Hawley & A. Jackson (Eds.), *Toward a common destiny: Educational perspectives on improving race and ethnic relations* (pp. 39–70). San Francisco: Jossey-Bass.

Heath, S. B., & Langman, J. (1994). Shared thinking and the register of coaching. In D. Biber & E. Finegan (Eds.), *Sociolinguistic perspectives on register* (pp. 82–105). Oxford: Oxford University Press.

Heath, S. B., & McLaughlin, M. W. (1993). *Identity and inner-city youth: Beyond ethnicity and gender.* New York: Teachers College Press.

Heath, S. B., & McLaughlin, M. W. (1994). Learning for anything everyday. *Journal of Curriculum Studies, 26*(5), 476–489.

Hoyle, S., & Adger, C. T. (Eds.). (1998). *Language practices of older children.* New York: Oxford University Press.

Jakobson, R. (1941). *Kindersprache.* Uppsala, Sweden: Almquist & Wiksells.

Kuczaj, S. A. (1983). *Crib speech and language play.* New York: Springer-Verlag.

Labov, W. (1972). *Language in the inner city: Studies in the black English vernacular.* Philadelphia: University of Pennsylvania Press.

Labov, W., Cohen, P., & Robins, C. (1965). *A preliminary study of the structure of English used by Negro and Puerto Rican speakers in New York City.* Co-operative Research Project 3091. Washington, DC: office of Education.

Labov, W., Cohen, P., Robins, C., & Lewis, J. (1968). *A study of the non-standard English of Negro and Puerto Rican speakers in New York City.* Report on Co-operative Research Project 3288. New York: Columbia University.

Labov, W., & Waletzky, J. (1967). Narrative analysis. In J. Helms (Ed.), *Essays on the verbal and visual arts* (pp. 12–44). Seattle: University of Washington Press.

Lave, J., & Wenger, E. (1991). *Situated learning: Legitimate peripheral participation.* New York: Cambridge University Press.

Lehrer, A. (1983). *Wine and conversation.* Bloomington: Indiana University Press.

Loban, W. D. (1963). *The language of elementary school children.* Champaign, IL: National Council of Teachers of English.

Males, M. A. (1996). *The scapegoat generation: America's war on adolescents.* Monroe, ME: Common Courage Press.

McElhinny, B. (1993). *We all wear the blue: Language, gender and police work.* Unpublished dissertation, Stanford University.

Mehan, H. (1979). *Learning lessons.* Cambridge, MA: Harvard University Press.

Miringoff, M. L. (1996). *1996 Index of social health.* Tarrytown, NY: Fordham Institute for Innovation in Social Policy.

Nelson, K. (Ed.). (1989). *Narratives from the crib.* Cambridge, MA: Harvard University Press.

Ntshanagase, D. K. (1995). Indaba yami i-straight: Language and language practices in Soweto. In R. Mesthrie (Ed.), *Language and social history: Studies in South African sociolinguistics* (pp. 291–297). Cape Town: David Philip.

Rampton, B. (1995). *Crossing: Language and ethnicity among adolescents.* London: Longman.

Rogoff, B. (1994). Developing understanding of the idea of communities of learners. *Mind, Culture, and Activity, 1*(4), 209–229.

Romaine, S. (1984). *The language of children and adolescents; The acquisition of communicative competence.* London: Blackwell.

Rose, M. (1989). *Lives on the boundary: The struggles and achievements of America's underprepared.* New York: Free Press.

Schieffelin, B. B., & Ochs, E. (Eds.). (1986a). *Language socialization across cultures.* New York: Cambridge University Press.

Schieffelin, B. B., & Ochs, E. (1986b). Language socialization. *Annual Review of Anthropology, 15,* 163–246.

Slobin, D. I. (1967). *A field manual for cross-cultural study of the acquisition of communicative competence.* Berkeley: University of California ACUC Bookstore.

Slobin, D. I. (1985a). *The crosslinguistic study of language acquisition. Vol. 1: The data.* Hillsdale, NJ: Lawrence Erlbaum Associates.

Slobin, D. I. (1985b). *The crosslinguistic study of language acquisition. Vol. 2: Theoretical issues.* Hillsdale, NJ: Lawrence Erlbaum Associates.

Snow, C. E., & Ferguson, C. A. (1977). *Talking to children: Language input and acquisition.* Cambridge, England: Cambridge University Press.

Spindler, G. (Ed.). (1963). *Education and culture.* New York: Holt, Rinehart & Winston.

Wax, M., Wax, R., & Dumont, R. V. (1964). *Formal education in an American Indian community.* Supplement to *Social Problems, 11*(4).

Weir, R. H. (1970). *Language in the crib.* The Hague, Netherlands: Mouton.

Chapter 4

Through the Eyes of Children: An Ethnographic Perspective on Neighborhoods and Child Development

Linda M. Burton
The Pennsylvania State University

Townsand Price-Spratlen
Ohio State University

> *The young child is often thought of as a little scientist exploring the world and discovering the principles of its operation. We often forget that while the scientist is working on the border of human knowledge and is finding out things that nobody yet knows, the child is finding out precisely what everybody knows.*
> —Newman (1982, p. 26, cited in Rogoff, 1990, p. 42)

In recent decades, intense scholarly and public policy debates concerning the geographic concentration of poverty (Coulton & Padney, 1992; Lewin-Epstein, 1985; Wilson, 1987), high-risks neighborhoods (Burton, 1991; Jencks & Mayer, 1990), and the ecology of human development (Bronfenbrenner, 1979; Garbarino & Crouter, 1978; Jessor & Jessor, 1973; Moen, Elder, & Luscher, 1995; Spencer, 1995; Wohlwill & Heft, 1987) have rekindled theoretical and methodological discourse on neighborhood context and child development (Brewster et al., 1993; Burton, Price-Spratlen, & Spencer, 1997; Furstenberg & Hughes, 1997; Garbarino & Sherman, 1980). This discourse continues to generate a broad range of conceptual and methodological approaches for studying neighborhood contexts and children (Gephart, 1997). For example, Jencks and Mayer (1990) in a comprehensive review of existing quantitative research on this topic, outlined four conceptual approaches that are currently used in neighborhood and child development research:

(1) the contagion model, which is concerned with the impact of neighborhood peer influences on the prevalence of child behavior problems in socioeconomic and racially homogeneous communities;

(2) the collective socialization model, which posits a relationship between child outcomes and the prevalence of neighborhood adults who can serve as role models and monitors of the behavior of neighborhood children;

(3) a resource model, which suggests that child outcomes are related to the level of resources (e.g., community centers, parks, medical care, daycare) available in neighborhoods; and

(4) a competition model, which argues that neighborhood effects on children are a function of community residents competing for scarce resources (Brooks-Gunn, Duncan, Klebanov, & Sealand, 1994; Crane, 1991; Furstenberg & Hughes, 1997; Sampson, 1992).

Comparable variety is noted in the methodological approaches used to assess neighborhoods. Approaches include windshield surveys (Spencer et al., 1997), block and block-group analysis of census data (Korbin & Coulton, 1997), and the use of surveys to determine residents' perceptions of risks in a specific geographic area (Hyson & Bolin, 1990).

Although existing conceptual and methodological approaches, such as those reviewed by Jencks and Mayer (1990), provide useful frameworks for the study of neighborhoods and child development, empirical explorations based on these approaches often render inconclusive findings concerning the impact of neighborhood context on child outcomes. In part, existing empirical research on neighborhoods and child development may be inconclusive because the conceptual and methodological frameworks used are rarely derived from children's perceptions of their neighborhood experiences (Jacobs, 1961; Proshansky & Fabian, 1987; Super & Harkness, 1986). Garbarino, Galambos, Plantz, and Kostelny (1993) note that neighborhoods are principally the territory or "turf" of children. Children define the physical boundaries of their "turf" and also develop shared meanings and impressions of the beliefs and behaviors that occur within those boundaries. As such, one can not truly assess the impact of neighborhoods on the development of children without first understanding the definitions and meanings children attach to their neighborhoods (Berg & Medrich, 1980; Bryant, 1985; Garbarino, Kostelny, & Dubrow 1991; Maurer & Baxter, 1972; Proctor, Volser, & Sirles, 1993).

A conceptual and methodological approach that is particularly useful for discerning children's experiences in neighborhoods, but that has not been used to its potential in recent research efforts, is ethnography (Burton, 1997; Clark, 1983; Furstenberg, 1993; Jarrett, 1990; Merry, 1981; Williams, 1981; Sullivan, 1989). Ethnographers use intensive, in-depth, inves-

tigative and analytic strategies (e.g., life-history interviews, participant observation, focus groups, field observation) to gather and analyze data on
the shared definitions, beliefs, practices, and behaviors of individuals within
a specific social context or culture (Becker, 1970; Denzin & Lincoln, 1994;
LeCompte & Preissle, 1993; Spradley & McCurdy, 1972; Suttles, 1976;
Swidler, 1986). As such, ethnographers are able to explore, in fine-grained
detail, children's subjective perceptions of neighborhoods, and are able,
through direct observation and participation in the activities of children
in these contexts, to identify the neighborhood dynamics and social processes that influence children's lives (Corsaro & Rosier, 1992; Korbin &
Coulton, 1997).

In this chapter, using ethnographic data from a 5-year community-based
study of children's and their families' experiences in neighborhoods, we
discuss four prevailing issues in existing neighborhood research that underscore the importance of incorporating the child's perspective in studies
of neighborhood influences and child development. First, we outline the
issues. Second, we provide a brief overview of our ethnographic study and
illustrate the importance of attending to these research issues as reflected
in the "voices" of children. And, third, we discuss the implications of
incorporating the child's perspective in future research on neighborhood
context and child development.

CONCEPTUAL AND METHODOLOGICAL ISSUES
IN THE STUDY OF NEIGHBORHOODS
AND CHILDREN

In reviewing the existing literature on neighborhoods and children, we
identified four key issues that underscore the importance of incorporating
the child's perspective in studies of neighborhood effects and developmental outcomes for children. The first issue concerns the conceptual
definition of neighborhood (Tienda, 1991). As indicated earlier, there are
a variety of conceptual and operational definitions of neighborhood
currently used in the study of context and child outcomes (Gephart, 1997).
The most frequently used definition is one in which neighborhoods are
defined as specific territorial or geographic sites (Bennett, 1993; Chaskin,
1994; Keller, 1968; Tepperman & Richardson, 1986). This definition, often
considered to be an objective delimiter of neighborhood, typically does
not incorporate the meaning of neighborhood boundaries as they are
defined by children (Allen et al., 1985; Bronfenbrenner, 1993; Guest &
Lee, 1984; Haney & Knowles, 1978; Hunter, 1974; Lewin, 1935).

Lee, Oropesa, and Kanan (1994) note that neighborhoods are not merely
"demarcated territorial units, but rather, they are social constructions named
and bounded differently by different individuals" (p. 249). This conceptu-

alization underscores the importance of considering subjective definitions of neighborhood, particularly in the study of context and child development. Children's cultural experiences and social constructions of neighborhood boundaries and experiences are often vastly different from the objective neighborhood delimiters imposed by social scientists and other adults (Berg & Medrich, 1980; Bryant, 1985; Garbarino et al., 1993; von Andel, 1990). Consequently, a lack of attention to children's subjective definitions of neighborhoods may result in both the collection and interpretation of data that do not accurately represent the relationship between neighborhood influences and developmental outcomes as experienced by the child (Elliott & Huizinga, 1990; Super & Harkness, 1986).

In a fair number of existing studies on neighborhoods and child outcomes, researchers have designated the geographic boundaries of neighborhoods according to census tracts (Sawicki & Flynn, 1996). These definitions give no attention to children's perceptions of their neighborhood boundaries. The use of census tract-level designations without consideration of children's definitions of boundaries has several limitations. First, census tracts constitute geographic units that are much larger than the developmental neighborhood niches of children. Second, the focus on census tracts as the unit of analysis for neighborhoods does not facilitate the exploration of the range of heterogeneous outcomes that exists in the smaller geographic units in which children live. Third, census tract delineations of neighborhoods are often based on the "social address" approach—that is, assessments of neighborhood effects are restricted to neighborhoods where the children reside rather than including the neighborhoods where children spend most of their time. Fourth, the representativeness of census data, particularly for ethnic–racial minorities, has consistently been challenged by social scientists and as such, raises questions concerning their generalizability in studying context and the lives of ethnic–minority children.

The second issue that is important to consider in the study of neighborhoods and child development concerns Bronfenbrenner's (1986) discussion of individual development and the "social address." The social address paradigm is limited to the assessment of developmental outcomes as they are related to the sociodemographic features (e.g., racial–ethnic composition; percentage of families living in poverty) of the geographic areas children reside in (Bronfenbrenner, 1986). Children are thus ascribed certain contextual experiences based on the social address of their current geographic residence. Bronfenbrenner and Crouter (1983) note that this paradigm has a number of limitations:

> [within this paradigm] No explicit consideration is given . . . to intervening structures or processes through which the environment might affect the course of development. One looks only at the social address—that is, the

environmental label—with no attention to what the environment is like, what people are living there, what they are doing, or how the activities taking place could affect the child. (pp. 361–362)

In addition to the limitations outlined by Bronfenbrenner and Crouter (1983), assigning social address labels to children, using the child's current geographic residence as the "locator" of a contextual experience, is particularly problematic in studying the lives of ethnic–racial minority children. In general, research on ethnic–minority families, particularly African Americans, suggests that family living arrangements are flexible and fluid. Families live coresidentially and extraresidentially, both within and across neighborhoods (Anderson, 1990; Burton & Jarrett, 1991; Martin & Martin, 1978; Price-Spratlen & Burton, 1995; Stack, 1974; Valentine, 1978). Holloman and Lewis (1978), in an ethnographic account of urban African American families, clearly illustrate this point in a profile of the residential dispersion of a family referred to as the "clan":

At present, nine households of the clan are located within a maximum of seven blocks of each other in the Uptown area. . . . Before the move Uptown by those now in the central cluster, the entire clan was located on the West Side of Chicago. Six households remain in three general locations, but are not in the same building. . . . Members of the core group who live away from the central cluster are still within walking distance of one other household. (pp. 230–231)

The work of Holloman and Lewis (1978), as well as others, suggests that using a single residential address as an identifier of the primary neighborhood in which a child develops may not provide an accurate view of the impact of neighborhoods on child outcomes (Aschenbrenner, 1975; Clark, 1983; Furstenberg, 1993; Jarrett, 1995; Silverstein & Krate, 1975; Stack & Burton, 1993; Williams & Kornblum, 1994; Zollar, 1985). Some children experience a multiplicity of "neighborhoods of residence." The developmental effects of the multiplicity of neighborhood residences are not captured in research that ascribes social address characteristics to a child using a child's single, currently reported address as an indicator of neighborhood membership.

In addition, the recent ethnographic work of Burton and Graham (in press) suggests that as children move into adolescence, considering the multiplicity of neighborhoods of residence is not sufficient for understanding the impact of context on development (Allison & Takei, 1993; Burton & Duncan, 1993). Burton and Graham's (in press) longitudinal community-based studies of urban African American teens suggest that adolescents engaged in the developmental process of individuation venture beyond the confines of their neighborhoods of residence and experience the influence of "other neighborhoods" through "hanging out" in these environments. They argue that these "other neighborhoods," termed "neighborhoods of sociability," are as, if not more, important to consider in the study of context and adolescent development (Burton & Graham, in press; Merriwether-deVries, 1994). Comparable perspectives are reflected in the neighborhood and adolescent development research of others (e.g., Noack & Silbereisen, 1988). The research of Stokols and Shumaker (1981) suggests that adolescents are less place-dependent with respect to their neighborhood of residence because their desired activities can be satisfied in alternative settings. Schiavo (1988), in a neighborhood study of suburban youths, indicated that, for adolescents, the role of the neighborhood of residence diminishes in importance in everyday life because of outside neighborhood relationships, mobility, and independence. It is plausible, then, that the effect of the neighborhood of sociability on development is a critical factor to consider as children become mobile adolescents.

A third issue in existing research on neighborhood effects and child development concerns children and neighborhoods as interdependent systems. This perspective suggests that neighborhoods and children reciprocally influence each other. Overton and Reese (1977) argue that:

> Man and environment reciprocally interact and exert formative influences on each other. The assumptive base of this relation is opposed to both static material reality and a static reality of inherent forms . . . man in this relation is an active system which transforms or assimilates other active systems (i.e., environmental systems), and on the basis of the activity accommodates or changes itself in conformance with the earlier transformation. Human behavior and its development can be described as a "shaping" process only to the extent that it is accepted that man actively shapes the environment so transformed. (pp. 15–16)

In contrast to the interdependent systems approach, much of the existing research on causal links between neighborhoods and child outcomes tests unidirectional models—that is, how neighborhoods influence children (neighborhood → child outcome). However, as the perspective of Overton and Reese suggests, children and neighborhoods are engaged in constant interaction to produce developmental outcomes (Bronfenbrenner, 1979). Although these interactions are invariably mediated by families, it seems equally important, when attempting to uncover child outcomes, to consider the effects that children have on neighborhoods (MacLeod, 1987; Ogbu, 1974; Sullivan, 1988).

The fourth issue involves the notion of neighborhood as a "contextual moment" (Burton, 1991). With the exception of several ethnographic accounts of the lives of children in urban neighborhoods (Furstenberg, 1993; Gans, 1962; Hagendorn & Macon, 1988; Hippler, 1971; Howell, 1973;

Kotlowitz, 1991; Moore, 1969; Williams & Kornblum, 1994), existing studies of neighborhoods and child development that rely on census tract data present static profiles of neighborhood characteristics as they influence the lives of children. Neighborhoods, however, are not static. They have temporal rhythms and dynamic "life cycles" of their own (Burton & Graham, in press; Guest, 1974). Merry (1981), in an ethnographic study of neighborhoods and crime, highlighted the differential temporal use of public spaces in neighborhoods by varying ethnic groups. Burton (1991), in another ethnographic study, found that variations in the temporal organization of activities (e.g., drug trafficking) in neighborhoods is directly related to the type of care and monitoring children receive.

Although neighborhoods are difficult to measure using standard survey research strategies, it is important that social scientists in conceptualizing and designing studies of context and child development have an appreciation for the dynamic, fluid nature of neighborhoods. Neighborhood constructs and measures should reflect more than an assessment of "contextual moments." Indeed, neighborhoods have a developmental trajectory of their own, and it is likely that the processes involved in that trajectory are what have the greatest impact on developmental outcomes for children.

CHILDREN'S PERCEPTIONS OF NEIGHBORHOODS: INSIGHTS FROM AN ETHNOGRAPHIC STUDY

Data and Methods

Data from a 5-year ethnographic study of the impact of neighborhood context on the life course of multigeneration urban African American families are now presented to further illustrate the importance of addressing, in the studies of neighborhood effects and child development, the four issues we have delineated. The study, which began in June 1989 and concluded in December 1994, was conducted in a Northeastern city where 51% of the population is African American. Data collection involved the systematic use of multiple qualitative strategies to identify prevailing community and family beliefs concerning the definitions of neighborhoods, neighborhood processes, and the life-course development of urban African American children, teens, and adults. Four qualitative data collection strategies were employed: field observation (community ethnography); focus groups; life-history interviews with children, teens and their families; and participant-observation in neighborhood and family activities.

Field observations were conducted over the 5-year period and involved observational assessments and discussions with adult, adolescent, and child residents in 18 neighborhoods. These assessments focused on residents' definitions of the boundaries of neighborhoods, their perceptions of the social milieu and culture of their neighborhood, and their assessment of how neighborhoods differentially influenced the lives of children, adolescents, and adults. In addition, direct observation of the temporal organization of neighborhood activities and rhythms was conducted (Burton & Graham, in press). This data collection strategy involved the researchers spending time in the 18 neighborhoods during various periods (7:00 a.m.–3:00 p.m.; 3:00 p.m.–11:00 p.m.; and 11:00 p.m.–7:00 a.m.) and recording observations of the activities of neighborhood residents (e.g., children playing; families sitting on the porch; drug sales and so forth).

The focus group strategy involved generating 14 groups of 4 to 6 African American community residents to discuss specific issues concerning the culture of neighborhoods and developmental outcomes for children, teens, and adults. Each of the focus group sessions was videotaped. Three of the groups involved female children aged 7–10, and two groups included male children aged 8–11. The remaining groups were organized as follows: three comprised adolescent and young adult females aged 15–21; two of the groups included midlife and elderly females aged 45–80; two were composed of adolescent and young adult males aged 16–21; and two involved midlife and elderly males aged 45–67. The groups represented a range of generational and socioeconomic strata and included members from each of the 18 neighborhoods studied.

In-depth life-history interviews were conducted with members of 186 multigeneration African American families residing in the community. These interviews explored the meaning of neighborhood context in the lives of family members and also identified family beliefs and perceptions of life-course development. The 186 families were distributed equally across four socioeconomic strata—persistently poor, working poor, transient poor, and working class. All of the families studied had children between the ages of 5 and 18 and resided in one or more neighborhoods. In addition to the indepth interviews, participant observation in neighborhood and family activities such as block parties, "sitting on the stoop," and engaging in children's play activities provided baseline data on the use of physical space and resources in neighborhoods by children and other family members.

Seven African American field researchers collected qualitative data from children and their families using these four strategies. The data generated were transcribed and then analyzed using the grounded theory approach (Glaser & Strauss, 1967). The grounded theory approach is a style of analyzing qualitative data using a specific coding scheme to generate a profile of conceptual themes and relationships among variables that emerge in the data (Strauss, 1987). Several themes concerning the children's experiences in their neighborhoods emerged in the qualitative data. These themes were consistent with the four issues highlighted in the previous section: defining neighborhood boundaries; neighborhoods and the "social address"; child and neighborhoods as interdependent systems; and neighborhoods and the "contextual moment."

Defining Neighborhoods

Our experiences interviewing and participating in the lives of the children involved in our ethnographic study clearly underscored the importance of incorporating children's subjective appraisals in definitions of neighborhood boundaries. In 56% of the cases in our ethnographic study, the boundaries that children and adolescents identified as encompassing their "neighborhood turf" were vastly different from the boundaries of neighborhoods described by adults. For example, when asked to describe the boundaries of his neighborhood, Kevin, an 8-year-old boy, commented:

> Well, my neighborhood is where all my best friends live. Eric lives on the corner of Anderson, Devon lives in the middle of the block on Tyree Street, and Jason lives at the end of the street on Beacon. . . . My neighborhood doesn't go past those streets either way. That's my neighborhood.

When Kevin's mother was asked to define her son's neighborhood she commented:

> I would say that the neighborhood is an area that is about 8 blocks north, 5 blocks south, to the west by the river, and to the east by the railroad tracks. I call this Kevin's neighborhood because that's as far as he can walk and be safe without me.

Comparing Kevin's definition of neighborhood to that of his mother's illustrates the fact that they had distinctly different criteria for defining neighborhood boundaries. Kevin defined the boundaries according to his friendship ties and his mother defined the boundaries according to her perceptions of the geographic territory that Kevin could safely maneuver in without her accompanying him. Kevin's criterion for establishing neighborhood boundaries is consistent with a "neighborhood as network approach" (Bryant, 1985; Mitchell, 1969; Oliver, 1988; Wellman, 1979; Wellman & Leighton, 1979), whereas Kevin's mother's delineation is indicative of a "neighborhood as perceived risks area" perspective (Burton, Price-Spratlen, & Spencer, 1997). These differences in conceptual starting points for defining neighborhoods were further reflected in Kevin's and his mother's descriptions of neighborhood street boundaries. When we compared the street boundaries of Kevin's definition of neighborhood to his mother's, we found that Kevin's mother delineated a geographic area that was much larger than the area specified by Kevin. In many respects, Kevin's mother's definition of *neighborhood* was more consistent with the social scientist's approach, whose definitions of neighborhoods are often much larger geographic areas than are the developmental niches of children.

Inconsistencies between parents' and children's specific definitions of neighborhood boundaries were notable in our study. These inconsistencies also prevailed, but to a lesser degree, when the definitions of parents residing in the same neighborhoods were examined. However, unlike their parents, children residing in the same neighborhood often shared consistent definitions of their neighborhood turf. Not only were children's boundaries consistent with one another, their assessments of neighborhood culture were comparable as well. The comparability in children's assessments of neighborhood culture was indicative of the elaborate strategies children developed for "passing down" their understanding of the neighborhood to younger children. The following discourse between Sharelle (age 9), Dante (age 7), and Kenya (age 9) illustrates:

Sharelle: I been knowing every since I was five about what be going on in our neighborhood ... about rules and who makes them ... about when you can be outside and when you can't. . . . My momma didn't teach me, huh Kenya, you showed me.

Kenya: Yeah, I learned it from sugababe, now we got the little rookie Dante to teach.

Dante: I'm getting an understanding but I'm gon keep it on the down low. We can't tell old people everything.

The dialogue among Sharelle, Kenya, and Dante highlights, once again, the different information base that children operate from in defining their neighborhoods. Moreover, it underscores the point that parents are not always privy to the "neighborhood world" of their children. Increasingly, social scientists have recognized that children's perceptions of their environments, as compared with their parents' perceptions, are uniquely important predictors of behavioral outcomes (Garbarino, Kostelny, & Dubrow, 1991; van Andel, 1990). Consequently, understanding the child's appraisal of the boundaries of neighborhood space and the culture within that space may provide valuable insights concerning the relationships that social scientists hypothesize exist between neighborhood context and the developmental outcomes of children (Lynch, 1977; Schiavo, 1988; Torrell & Biel, 1985).

Neighborhoods and the "Social Address"

We noted earlier in our discussion that previous ethnographic research suggests that some children experience a "multiplicity of residences"—that is, children may be members of families who simultaneously coreside across multiple households located both within and across a variety of neighborhoods. As such, using a "social address" model in assessing the impact of neighborhood context on child outcomes may be particularly inappropriate for studying the lives of these children. Our ethnographic data support this contention. Consistent with other ethnographic studies (see Jarrett, 1990, 1998, for a comprehensive review), one third of the children in our study simultaneously resided in 2–4 households across several distinct neighborhoods. These children offered valuable insights into how their memberships in different neighborhoods influenced their behaviors as well as how they were perceived by others. Dwight, an 11-year-old who resided 2 days a week with his mother in a poor, high-risk neighborhood and 5 days a week with his grandmother in a stable, working-class neighborhood, had this to say:

> Lady, I think you're pretty smart so let me tell you how it is. When I go to my momma's I have to be a bad ass or I will get beat up. So if you see me over there, I look like that. But when I'm with Nana (grandmother) I'm another way 'cause the kids over there don't fight that much so I don't have to swell up (act like he's tough). . . . I go to school at Nana's but we don't give them my momma's address. You know why?

Eric, Dwight's 12-year-old friend, addresses this question:

> You never tell teachers your address if your momma live in a bad neighborhood 'cause they think you be like all the knuckleheads where your momma live even if you don't be there all the time . . . even if you live somewhere else most of the time . . . they still be trying to make you like them knuckleheads just cause they think that's where you be most of the time.

Both Dwight's and Eric's comments speak to the issue of the inappropriateness of using a "social address" model in assessing the impact of neighborhoods on children's lives. More importantly, however, their comments underscore the relevance of incorporating, in any interpretations of their developmental outcomes, children's astute perceptions of how neighborhoods influence them. Wylene, a 10-year-old who resides in three households, reinforces this point:

> People be studying me and everything and they think they know about me and how I live. They don't know nothing cause they don't pay attention to what I say. I live in three places and I'm different in every one. Each place makes me different. I know that. Why don't my teachers and counselors figure it out too?

Neighborhoods and Children as Interdependent Systems

Neighborhoods influence children, but, children also influence neighborhoods. Forty-three percent of our children articulated an intuitive understanding of this relationship and expressed their understanding to us. Devon, an 8-year-old, noted:

> I know I have to do my part to make the neighborhood a good place for
> all the little kids who play around here . . . so me and my friends pick up
> all the trash on the playground over there so it can be nice for them.

Tyrec, age 12, stated:

> My neighborhood so bad is cause some of the young bloods here is bad.
> Just cause it's all junky round here don't mean people in it got to be junky
> on the inside. If young brothers round here get together, we could make
> it a good place. Some my friends don't know that it be bad here cause they
> be bad not cause the neighborhood make them bad.

Devon's and Tyrec's views are representative of the feelings of reciprocity
toward their neighborhoods that a number of children in our study had.
Children's recognition of this reciprocity suggests the importance of adopt-
ing an "interdependent systems" approach in exploring the relationships
between neighborhoods and child outcomes. Clearly, if the researcher's
goal is to understand the impact of neighborhoods on child outcomes, it
seems equally important to discern how children, through their own actions, shape the environments in which they develop.

Neighborhoods and the "Contextual Moment"

In our research site the systematic observation of neighborhood and child
activities during various times of the day provided a dynamic perspective
on the ways in which children organize their behaviors around the temporal
rhythms of neighborhoods. For example, in six of the neighborhoods we
studied, we observed that children and their caregivers organized their
behaviors around illicit-drug trade "shifts" that occurred throughout the
day. Three distinct drug activity shifts operated in these neighborhoods:
a morning shift (7:00 a.m.–4:00 p.m.), an afternoon/evening shift (4:00
p.m.–10:00 p.m.), and a night shift (10:00 p.m.–6:00 a.m.) (Burton &
Graham, in press).

The morning shift is best described as having low levels of drug activity
and the dangers, such as crime, that accompany it. Parents and children who
participated in the study indicated that this was the time of day when most
drug dealers and users slept. Consequently, neighborhood residents who
were not involved in the local drug trade (which is the majority of families)
used the safe morning hours to do their grocery shopping and banking, visit
with friends in the neighborhood, attend church activities, deliver and pick
up children from school, and take toddlers and preschool children out for
walks. Parents and children described this as the "family time of day."

At approximately 4:00 p.m., the neighborhood "climate" changed.
Around this time, the small-time drug dealers opened for business on

neighborhood corners. Older residents, parents not involved in the local drug economy, and their children retreated to their homes. Young children and adolescents who had no adult supervision "hung out" on the streets. The local automobile traffic increased dramatically as people who lived outside the neighborhood stopped on their way home from work to purchase drugs. Uniformed police officers were nowhere to be found. Parents and children called this the "p.m. shift."

At 10:00 p.m., the neighborhoods underwent yet another transformation. Hard-core drug dealers made their appearance on the street. Young adult, heavily addicted drug users lay around, seemingly dead, in alleys and doorways of churches and local businesses. The presence of undercover police officers was easily discernible. In many respects, this is the most dangerous time of day in drug-plagued neighborhoods. Some of the children in our study who were awake to experience this time of day called it "the night shift."

In our study, we paid particular attention to the impact of the temporal organization of drug trade in these six neighborhoods on the child care that older children provided for their younger siblings. For example, a few of the older siblings (age 10–14) who were responsible for the care of younger children hung out on the street from 4:00 p.m. to 9:00 p.m.— the time of day when children on the streets were exposed to heightened dangers related to the drug economy, including increased automobile traffic and street fighting. It was quite common to see young children and adolescent child-care providers being solicited by small-time dealers to buy or sell drugs. When we asked Walter—a 14-year-old who was babysitting for his three younger siblings on a street corner—what impact the neighborhood drug activity had on his child-care responsibilities, he said: "I'm out here learning them the streets. Just 'cuz I got to watch my sisters and brother don't mean I got to stay inside with them."

Walter's comments point to the importance of understanding that children see the temporal organization of activities in their neighborhoods as opportunities to engage in certain behaviors. Clearly, children experience neighborhood influences as dynamic and not as "contextual moments." Thus, as social scientists move toward understanding the features of neighborhoods that impact child development, it becomes increasingly important to discern how the temporal organization and rhythms of neighborhoods affect the opportunities created for child development and the constraints placed on it.

DISCUSSION AND CONCLUSION

The purpose of this chapter was to discuss four conceptual and methodological issues pertaining to existing research on neighborhoods and child development as those issues relate to children's experiences in their communities. The four issues are: defining neighborhood boundaries; neighborhoods and the social address perspective; children and neighborhoods as interdependent systems; and neighborhoods and the "contextual moment." Using data from an ethnographic study of neighborhoods, children, and their families, our goal in discussing these issues was to demonstrate the importance of incorporating the child's perspective in studies of neighborhood influences and child development.

Our discussion suggests that social scientists and other adults may perceive neighborhoods differently than do children (Huckfeldt, 1983; van Vliet, 1981). However, the conceptual and methodological approaches used in child and neighborhood research typically focus on aspects of the adult neighborhood experience that children have limited interest in (Huckfeldt, 1983; Warren, 1978). As noted in the case of Kevin and his mother, the children define neighborhoods according to their friend network, whereas the mothers define neighborhoods according to their perception of risks. Each perspective would provide distinctly different interpretations of the relationships between neighborhood influences and child outcomes.

Given the distinct importance of incorporating children's perspectives on neighborhoods in child outcomes research, Hyson and Bolin (1990) suggested a variety of methodological strategies for assessing children's neighborhood experiences. For example, field observations of how children use neighborhood environments have provided rich, detailed data on how children perceive their communities (Lynch, 1977). Interviewing children about their environment during a concrete physical task such as a walk around the neighborhood is another useful strategy (Bryant, 1985). Asking children to draw maps or create models of their neighborhoods and then analyzing these products for content and style is a third strategy proposed by Hyson and Bollin (1990). Children's neighborhood appraisals may also be studied by asking them to comment on videotapes, pictures, or hypothetical situations about their neighborhoods. As children approach adolescence, structured rating scales, such as the Environmental Rating Scale (Bunting & Cousins, 1985) and the Semantic Differential Measure of Environmental Hazards (Golant & Burton, 1976) also can be administered.

The key issue is that the child's appraisal of his or her environment, as distinct from the appraisal of researchers, is an important factor to address in studying the relationship between neighborhood influences and child outcomes. Specifically, taking the child's perspective in light of the issues we have discussed allows the researcher to attend to four matters: (a) the geographic boundaries of neighborhoods become "developmentally and temporally anchored" for the child; (b) the fluidity of the child's neighborhood experiences beyond his or her residential address can be determined; (c) the interdependent relationship between neighborhood context and child behaviors can be assessed; and (d) the "rituals of daily life" that children participate in according to the temporal rhythms of neighborhoods can be more readily identified.

In a commentary on neighborhoods and human needs, Mead (cited in Garbarino et al. 1993) challenges adults to do the following:

> In building a neighborhood that meets human needs, we start with the needs of infants. These give us the groundwork on which we can build for contact with other human beings, with the physical environment, with the living world, and with the experiences through which the individual's full humanity can be realized. For every culture, the criteria must be modified. We cannot set our sights too low. But we can aim at the height, for we have as yet scarcely begun to explore human potentialities. How these are developed will depend on learning experiences we can provide for children through the human inhabitate in which they live. (p. 210)

We conclude with an extension of Mead's argument as it was voiced by one of the children in our study:

> The adults in our neighborhood always think they know what is best for us. They think they know how to build playgrounds and make this a nice place to grow up. The only problem is, they never ask us what we think about it. They just don't know what we know.

ACKNOWLEDGMENTS

The research reported in this paper was supported by grants to Linda Burton from the William T. Grant Foundation, a FIRST Award from the National Institute of Mental Health (No. R29MH 4605-01) and support services provided by the Population Research Institute, The Pennsylvania State University, which has core support from NICHD Grant 1-HD28263; and by a NIA Post-Doctoral Fellowship (T32AG 00208) to Townsand Price-Spratlen.

REFERENCES

Allen, H. M., Bentler, P. M., & Gutek, B. A. (1985). Probing theories of individual well-being: A comparison of quality-of-life models assessing neighborhood satisfaction. *Basic and Applied Social Psychology, 6*(3), 181–203

Allison, K., & Takei, Y. (1993). Diversity: The cultural contexts of adolescents and their families. In R. M. Lerner (Ed.), *Early adolescence: Perspectives on research, policy, and intervention* (pp. 51–69). Hillsdale, NJ: Lawrence Erlbaum Associates.

Anderson, E. (1990). *Streetwise: Race, class, and change in an urban community.* Chicago: University of Chicago Press.

Aschenbrenner, J. (1975). *Lifelines: Black families in Chicago.* New York: Holt, Rinehart & Winston.

Becker, H. S. (1970). *Sociological work: Method and substance.* Chicago: Aldine.

Bennett, L. (1993). Rethinking neighborhoods, neighborhood research, and neighborhood policy: Lessons from uptown. *Journal of Urban Affairs, 15*(3), 245–257.

Berg, M., & Medrich, E. A. (1980). Children in four neighborhoods. *Environment and Behavior, 12,* 320–348.

Brewster, K. L., Billy, J. O. G., & Grady, W. R. (1993). Social context and adolescent behavior: The impact of community on the transition to sexual activity. *Social Forces, 71,* 713–740.

Bronfenbrenner, U. (1979). *The ecology of human development.* Cambridge, MA: Harvard University Press.

Bronfenbrenner, U. (1986). *Ecology of the family as a context for human development.* Cambridge, MA: Harvard University Press.

Bronfenbrenner, U. (1993). The ecology of cognitive development: Research models and fugitive findings. In R. H. Wozniak & K. W. Fischer (Eds.), *Development in context.* Hillsdale, NJ: Lawrence Erlbaum Associates.

Bronfenbrenner, U., & Crouter, A. C. (1983). The evolution of environmental models in developmental research. In W. P. Kessen (Ed.), *History, theory, and methods: Vol. 1. Handbook of child psychology* (4th ed.). New York: Wiley.

Brooks-Gunn, J., Duncan, G. J., Klebanov, P. K., & Sealand, N. (1994). Do neighborhoods influence child and adolescent development? *American Journal of Sociology, 99,* 353–395.

Bryant, B. K. (1985). *The neighborhood walk: Sources of support in middle childhood.* Chicago: University of Chicago Press.

Burton, L. M. (1991). Caring for children: Drug shifts and their impact on families. *American Enterprise, 2,* 34–37.

Burton, L. M. (1997). Ethnography and the meaning of adolescence in high-risk neighborhoods. *Ethos, 25,* 208–217.

Burton, L. M., Allison, K., & Obeidallah, D. (1995). Social context and adolescence: Perspectives on development among inner-city African-American teens. In L. Crockett & A. C. Crouter (Eds.), *Pathways through adolescence: Individual development in relation to social context.* Hillsdale, NJ: Lawrence Erlbaum Associates.

Burton, L., & Duncan, G. J. (1993, April). *Effects of residential mobility on adolescent behavior.* Paper presented at the biennial meeting of the Society for Research in Child Development, New Orleans, LA.

Burton, L. M., & Graham, J. (in press). Neighborhood rhythms and the social activities of adolescent mothers. In R. Larson & A. C. Crouter (Eds.), *Temporal rhythms in adolescence: Clocks, calendars, and the coordination of daily life.* San Francisco: Jossey-Bass.

Burton, L., & Jarrett, R. L. (1991, August). *Studying African American family structure and process in underclass neighborhoods: Conceptual considerations.* Paper presented at the annual meeting of the American Sociological Association, Cincinnati, OH.

Burton, L. M., Price-Spratlen, T., & Spencer, M. B. (1997). On ways of thinking about measuring neighborhoods: Implications for studying context and developmental outcomes for children. In G. Duncan, J. Brooks-Gunn, & L. Aber (Eds.), *Neighborhood poverty: Context and consequences for children* (Vol. 1, pp. 132–144). New York: Russell Sage.

Chaskin, R. J. (1994). *Defining neighborhoods.* A background paper for the neighborhood mapping project of the Annie E. Casey Foundation.

Clark, R. M. (1983). *Family life and school achievement: Why poor black children succeed or fail.* Chicago: University of Chicago Press.

Corsaro, W. A., & Rosier, K. B. (1992). Documenting productive and reproductive processes in children's lives: Transition narratives of a black family living in poverty. In W. A. Corsaro

& P. J. Miller (Eds.), *Interpretive approaches to children's socialization: New directions for child development* (pp. 67–91). San Francisco: Jossey-Bass.

Coulton, C. J., & Padney, S. (1992). Geographic concentration of poverty and risk to children in urban neighborhoods. *American Behavioral Scientist, 35*, 238–257.

Crane, J. (1991). The epidemic theory of ghettos and neighborhood effects on dropping out and teenage child bearing. *American Journal of Sociology, 96*, 1126–1260.

Craven, P., & Wellman, B. (1973). The network city. *Sociological Inquiry, 43*, 57–88.

Denzin, N. K., & Lincoln, Y. S. (Eds.). (1994). *Handbook of qualitative research.* Thousand Oaks, CA: Sage.

Downs, A. (1981). *Neighborhoods and urban development.* Washington, DC: The Brookings Institute.

Elliott, D. S., & Huizinga, D. (1990, August). *The mediating effects of the social structure in high-risk neighborhoods.* Paper presented at the annual meeting of the American Sociological Association, Washington, DC.

Emirbayer, M., & Goodwin, J. (1994). Network analysis, culture, and the problem of agency. *American Journal of Sociology, 99*(6), 1411–1454.

Fischer, C. S. (1982). *To dwell among friends: Personal networks in town and city.* Chicago: University of Chicago Press.

Fischer, C. S., Jackson, R. M., Stueve, C. A., Gerson, K., McCallister-Jones, L., & Baldassare, M. (1977). *Networks and places: Social relations in the urban setting.* New York: The Free Press.

Furstenberg, F. F., Jr. (1993). How families manage risk and opportunity in dangerous neighborhoods. In W. J. Wilson (Ed.), *Sociology and the public agenda* (pp. 231–258). Newbury Park, CA: Sage.

Furstenberg, F. F., Jr., & Hughes, M. (1997). The influence of neighborhoods on children's development: A theoretical perspective and research agenda. In J. Brooks-Gunn, G. Duncan, & L. Aber (Eds.), *Neighborhood poverty: Context and consequences for children* (Vol. 1). New York: Russell Sage.

Gans, H. J. (1962). *The urban villagers.* New York: Free Press.

Garbarino, J., & Crouter, A. (1978). Defining the community context for parent-child relations: The correlates of child maltreatment. *Child Development, 49*, 604–616.

Garbarino, J., Galambos, N. L., Plantz, M. C., & Kostelny, K. (1993). The territory of childhood. In J. Garbarino (Ed.), *Children and families in the social environment* (2nd ed., pp. 201–229). New York: Aldine de Gruyter.

Garbarino, J., & Sherman, D. (1980). High risk neighborhoods and high risk families: The human ecology of child maltreatment. *Child Development, 51*, 188–198.

Garbarino, J., Kostelny, K., & Dubrow, N. (1991). What children can tell us about living in danger. *American Psychologist, 46*(4), 376–383.

Gephart, M. (1997). Neighborhoods and communities as contexts for development. In J. Brooks-Gunn, G. J. Duncan, & J. L. Aber (Eds.), *Neighborhood poverty: Context and consequences for children* (Vol. 1, pp. 1–43). New York: Russell Sage Foundation Press.

Glaser, B., & Strauss, A. (1967). *The discovery of grounded theory.* Chicago: Aldine.

Guest, A. M. (1974). Neighborhood life cycles and social status. *Economic Geography, 50*, 228–243.

Guest, A. M., & Lee, B. A. (1984). How urbanites define their neighborhoods. *Population and Environment, 7*, 32–56.

Hagedorn, J., & Macon, P. (1988). *People and folks: Gangs and the underclass in a Rustbelt city.* Chicago: Lake View Press.

Haney, W. G., & Knowles, E. S. (1978). Perceptions of neighborhoods by city and suburban residents. *Human Ecology, 6*(2), 201–214.

Hannerz, U. (1969). *Soulside: Inquiries into ghetto culture and community.* New York: Columbia University Press.

Hart, R. (1979). The spatial world of the child. In W. Michelson, S. V. Levine, & E. Michelson (Eds.), *The child in the city* (pp. 102–116). Toronto: University of Toronto Press.

Hill, M. (1989). The role of social networks in the care of young children. *Children and Society, 3*(3), 195–211.

Hippler, A. E. (1971). *Hunter's Point: A black ghetto.* New York: Basic Books.

Holloman, R. E., & Lewis, F. E. (1978). The "clan": Case study of a black extended family in Chicago. In D. Shimkin, E. Shimkin, & D. A. Frate (Eds.), *The extended family in black societies* (pp. 201–238). The Hague, Netherlands: Mouton.

Howell, J. (1973). *Hard living on Clay Street.* Garden City, NY: Anchor Books.

Hyson, M. C., & Bollin, G. G. (1990). Children's appraisals of home and neighborhood risks: Questions for the 1990s. *Children's Environment Quarterly, 7*(3), 50–60.

Huckfeldt, R. R. (1983). Social contexts, social networks, and urban neighborhoods: Environmental constraints on friendship choice. *American Journal of Sociology, 89,* 651–669.

Hunter, A. (1974). *Symbolic communities: The persistence and change of Chicago's local communities.* Chicago: University of Chicago Press.

Jacobs, J. (1961). *The death and life of great American cities.* New York: Vintage.

Jarrett, R. L. (1990). *A comparative examination of socialization patterns among low-income African-Americans, Chicanos, Puerto Ricans, and whites: A review of the ethnographic literature.* New York: Social Science Research Council.

Jarrett, R. L. (1995). Growing up poor: The family experiences of socially mobile youth in low-income African-American neighborhoods. *Journal of Adolescent Research, 10,* 111–135.

Jarrett, R. L. (1998). African-American children, families, and neighborhoods: Qualitative contributions to understanding developmental pathways. *Applied Developmental Science, 2,* 2–16.

Jencks, C., & Mayer, S. E. (1990). The social consequences of growing up in a poor neighborhood. In L. E. Lynn, Jr., & M. G. H. McGeary (Eds.), *Inner-city poverty in the United States* (pp. 111–186). Washington, DC: National Academy Press.

Jessor, R., & Jessor, S. L. (1973). The perceived environment in behavioral science. *American Behavioral Scientist, 16*(6), 801–827.

Keller, S. (1968). *The urban neighborhood.* New York: Random House.

Korbin, J. E., & Coulton, C. J. (1997). Understanding the neighborhood context for children and families: Combining epidemiological and ethnographic approaches. In J. Brooks-Gunn, G. J. Duncan, & J. L. Aber (Eds.), *Neighborhood poverty: Context and consequences for children* (Vol. 2). New York: Russell Sage Foundation.

Kotlowitz, A. (1991). *There are no children here.* New York: Anchor.

LeCompte, M. D., & Preissle, J. (Eds.). (1993). *Ethnography and qualitative design in educational research* (2nd ed.). New York: Academic Press.

Lee, B. A., Oropesa, R. S., & Konan, J. W. (1994). Neighborhood context and residential mobility. *Demography, 31,* 249–270.

Lewin, K. (1935). *A dynamic theory of personality.* New York: McGraw-Hill.

Lewin-Epstein, N. (1985). Neighborhoods, local labor markets, and employment opportunities for white and non-white youth. *Social Science Quarterly, 66,* 163–171.

Lynch, K. (Ed.). (1977). *Growing up in cities.* Cambridge, MA: MIT Press.

Martin, E., & Martin, J. (1978). *The black extended family.* Chicago, IL: University of Chicago Press.

MacLeod, J. (1987). *Ain't no making it.* Boulder, CO: Westview.

Maurer, R., & Baxter, J. C. (1972). Images of the neighborhood and city among Black-, Anglo-, and Mexican-American children. *Environment and Behavior, 4*(4), 351–387.

Mayer, S. E., & Jenks, C. (1989). Growing up in poor neighborhoods: How much does it matter? *Science, 243,* 1441–1445.

Merriwether-deVries, C. (1994). *Exploring the relationship between neighborhood quality and adolescent depression among urban resident adolescents.* Unpublished masters thesis, The Pennsylvania State University.

Merry, S. E. (1981). *Urban danger: Life in a neighborhood of strangers.* Philadelphia: Temple University Press.

Moen, P., Elder, G. H., & Luscher, K. (1995). *Examining lives in context.* Washington, DC: American Psychological Association.

Moore, W. (1969). *The vertical ghetto: Everyday life in an urban project.* New York: Random House.

Mitchell, J. C. (1969). The concept and use of social networks. In J. C. Mitchell (Ed.), *Social networks in urban situations* (pp. 1–50). Manchester, England: University of Manchester Press.

Myers, H. F. (1989). Urban stress and mental health in black youth: An epidemiological and conceptual update. In R. L. Jones (Ed.), *Black adolescents* (pp. 123–154). Berkeley, CA: Cobb & Henry.

Newman, D. (1982). Perspective-taking versus content in understanding lies. *Quarterly Newsletter of the Laboratory of Comparative Human Cognition, 4,* 26–29.

Noack, P., & Silbereisen, R. K. (1988). Adolescent development and the choice of leisure settings. *Children's Environments Quarterly, 5,* 25–33.

Ogbu, J. (1974). *The next generation: An ethnography of education in an urban neighborhood.* New York: Academic Press.

Oliver, M. L. (1988). The urban black community as network: Toward a social network perspective. *The Sociological Quarterly, 29,* 623–645.

Overton, W., & Reese, H. W. (1977). General models for man-environment relations. In H. McGurk (Ed.), *Ecological factors in human development* (pp. 11–20). New York: Elsevier North-Holland.

Price-Spratlen, T., & Burton, L. M. (1995). *Theoretical models and the 'hood: Considering the effect of research strategies on our understanding of African-American neighborhoods.* Paper presented at the annual meeting of the Population Association of America, San Francisco, CA.

Proctor, E. K., Volser, N. R., & Sirles, E. A. (1993). The social-environmental context of child clients: An empirical exploration. *Social Work, 38*(3), 256–262.

Proshansky, H. M., & Fabian, A. K. (1987). The development of place identity in the child. In C. S. Weinstein & T. G. David (Eds.), *Spaces for children.* New York: Plenum.

Rogoff, B. (1990). *Apprenticeship in thinking.* New York: Oxford University Press.

Sampson, R. J. (1992). Family management and child development: Insights from social disorganization theory. In J. McCord (Ed.), *Advances in criminological theory* (Vol. 3, pp. 63–93). New Brunswick, NJ: Transaction Books.

Sawicki, D. S., & Flynn, P. (1996). Neighborhood indicators: A review of the literature and assessment of conceptual and methodological issues. *Journal of American Planning, 62,* 165–183.

Schiavo, S. R. (1988). Age differences in assessment and use of a suburban neighborhood among children and adolescents. *Children's Environment Quarterly, 5*(2), 4–9.

Silverstein, B., & Krate, R. (1975). *Children of the dark ghetto: A developmental psychology.* New York: Praeger.

Spencer, M. B (1995). Old issues and new theorizing about African American youth: A phenomenological variant of ecological systems theory. In R. L. Taylor (Ed.), *Black youth: Perspectives on their status in the United States.* Westport, CT: Praeger.

Spencer, M. B., McDermott, P. A., Burton, L. M., & Kochman, T. J. (1997). An alternative approach to assessing neighborhood effects on early adolescent achievement and problem behavior. In G. Duncan, J. Brooks-Gunn, & L. Aber (Eds.), *Neighborhood poverty: Context and consequences for children* (Vol. 1, pp. 45–157). New York: Russell Sage.

Spradley, J. P., & McCurdy, D. W. (1972). *The cultural experience: Ethnography in complex society.* Chicago: Science Research Associates.

Stack, C. B. (1974). *All our kin: Survival strategies in a black community.* New York: Harper & Row.

Stack, C. B., & Burton, L. M. (1993). Kinscripts. *Journal of Comparative Family Studies, 24,* 157–170.

Stokols, D., & Shumaker, S. A. (1981). People in places: A transactional view of settings. In J. Harvey (Ed.), *Cognition, social behavior, and the environment.* Hillsdale, NJ: Lawrence Erlbaum Associates.

Strauss, A. (1987). *Qualitative analysis for social scientists.* Cambridge, England: Cambridge University Press.

Sullivan, M. (1989). *Getting paid: Youth, crime, and work in the inner-city.* Ithaca, NY: Cornell University Press.

Super, C. M., & Harkness, S. (1986). The developmental niche: A conceptualization at the interface of child and culture. *International Journal of Behavioral Development, 9,* 545–569.

Suttles, G. D. (1976). Urban ethnography: Situational and normative accounts. *Annual Review of Sociology, 2,* 1–8.

Swidler, A. (1986). Culture in action: Symbols and strategies. *American Sociological Review, 51,* 273–286.

Tepperman, L., & Richardson, R. J. (1986). *The social world: An introduction to sociology.* Toronto: McGraw-Hill Ryerson.

Tienda, M. (1991). Poor people and poor places: Deciphering neighborhood effects on poverty outcomes. In J. Huber (Ed.), *Macro-micro linkages in sociology.* Newbury Park, CA: Sage.

Torrell, G., & Biel, A. (1985). Parental restrictions and children's acquisition of neighborhood knowledge. In T. Garling & J. Valsiner (Eds.), *Children within environments: Toward a psychology of accident prevention* (pp. 107–118). New York: Plenum.

Valentine, B. L. (1978). *Hustling and other hard work: Lifestyles in the ghetto.* New York: The Free Press.

van Vliet, W. (1981). Neighborhood evaluations by city and suburban children. *Journal of the American Planners Association, 47*(4), 458–466.

von Andel, J. (1990). Places children like, dislike, and fear. *Children's Environment Quarterly, 7*(4), 24–31.

Wellman, B. (1979). The community question: The intimate networks of East Yorkers. *American Journal of Sociology, 84,* 1201–1231.

Wellman, B., & Leighton, B. (1979). Networks, neighborhoods, and communities: Approaches to the study of the community question. *Urban Affairs Quarterly, 14,* 363–390.

Williams, M. (1981). *On the street where I lived.* New York: Holt, Rinehart & Winston.

Williams, T., & Kornblum, W. (1994). *The uptown kids: Struggle and hope in the projects.* New York: Putnam.

Wilson, W. J. (1987). *The truly disadvantaged: The inner city, the underclass and public policy.* Chicago: University of Chicago Press.

Wohlwill, J. F., & Heft, H. (1987). The physical environment and the development of the child. In D. Stokols & I. Altman (Eds.), *Handbook of environmental psychology* (Vol. 1, pp. 281–328). New York: Wiley.

Zollar, A. C. (1985). *A member of the family: Strategies for black family continuity.* Chicago: Nelson-Hall.

Chapter 5

Cultural Processes in Child Competence: How Rural Caribbean Parents Evaluate Their Children

Eric H. Durbrow
The Pennsylvania State University

BACKGROUND

As evident from the contributions in this volume and elsewhere, psychologists have expanded the cultural contexts of their models of development (e.g., Bornstein et al., 1996; Rogoff & Morelli, 1989; Saxe, 1991) while anthropologists and ethnologists have recently proposed approaches integrating culture, biology, and development (e.g., Chisholm, 1993; Draper & Harpending, 1987; Worthman, 1992).[1] This renewed interest may be due to the recent zeitgeist of multiculturalism and globalism, as well as the realization of the limits of developmental models neglecting cultural processes.

Psychologists and anthropologists bring to the study of child development two powerful tools: longitudinal research design and community-centered fieldwork. Developmental psychologists and psychiatrists have conducted dozens of birth-to-adulthood studies (e.g., Masten, 1989; Rutter & Quinton, 1984; Sameroff & Seifer, 1990; Silva, 1990; Werner & Smith, 1989), improving our understanding of how children mature, how vulner-

---

[1]Throughout this chapter, I use *anthropologist* and *psychologist* loosely. Many scholars, such as Shweder or Super, are not so easily categorized into one or the other role. Nevertheless, I will not let the fact that some psychologists do anthropology and some anthropologists do psychology interfere with distinctions I draw between psychological and anthropological approaches.

able they are to early trauma, and what helps them overcome challenges across the life span. Anthropologists, in contrast, become more familiar with their subjects but typically over less of their life span. By spending a year or more living with the people they study, fieldworkers have documented childhood in non-Western and nonindustrialized communities. By taking many "snapshots" of individuals over many years and long "video clips" of individuals at one particular time, psychologists and anthropologists provide complementary observations describing child's development across the life span and across cultures.

Despite their common interest in child development, psychologists and anthropologists tend to approach their subjects quite differently. Psychologists usually concentrate on the etic perspective. They describe and explain behaviors they observe using concepts and categories they have devised (e.g., "prosocial behavior" or "parallel play") and that may not be meaningful to the people they study. They usually remain cultural outsiders— independent from the people they study. Only recently have articles in *Developmental Psychology* and *Child Development* considered, almost as an afterthought, how parents in non-Western societies account for their children and their development (e.g., Shwalb, Shwalb, & Shoji, 1994; Yang, Ollendick, Dong, Xia, & Lin, 1995).

For sociocultural anthropologists, on the other hand, an insider or emic perspective is their *raison d'être*. By "thinking through others" (Shweder, 1991), anthropologists attempt to become cultural insiders (though none succeed). For example, while a psychologist may claim that a Yąnomamö child is crying because he is experiencing attachment separation, an anthropologist may adopt the Yąnomamö perspective describing the child as changing into *no uhudi*, acquiring a soul (Chagnon, 1983). Both approaches, the etic and the emic, are important. The etic approach more easily allows for comparative analyses leading to generalizations about behavior and development across contexts. Yet given the diversity of contexts, these transcultural generalizations are likely to have limits. The emic approach enables researchers to understand culturally specific motives and ways of thinking but often makes comparative analysis more difficult.

Although some studies include both approaches (e.g., Crystal & Stevenson, 1995), researchers usually adopt one approach or the other. The result of this specialization is evident by the rarity of emic-oriented studies in developmental journals and by the dismissal of psychological universals in some versions of cultural psychology (Shweder, 1990; see also, Schwartz, 1992; Spiro, 1984; Worthman, 1992). Although developmental psychologists have erected grand theories of development based on studies of a minority of the world's children or have exported their concepts to studies of non-Western people—Kagitçibasi (1995) refers to this "as looking West for theory and East for data"—sociocultural anthropologists have become myopically preoccupied with ethnographic storytelling often missing the forest for the trees. Is this gap likely to remain or widen? What areas of inquiry can draw developmental psychologists and sociocultural anthropologists together?

The purpose of this chapter is to show how inquiry into criteria of child competence may help broaden the overlap between the two approaches. Concentrating on the emic aspects of child competence, I discuss its etiology, function, and why it is of interest to psychologists as well as anthropologists. To illustrate research in child competence criteria, I present results from two field studies in the East Caribbean. I then discuss how emic-oriented research in child competence provides a basis for better integrating cultural and developmental processes, the theme of this Minnesota Symposium.

PARENTAL BELIEFS ABOUT CHILD COMPETENCE

Research examining the beliefs parents have about children and parenting has blossomed during the 1990s. For example, Bornstein et al. (1996) examined differences in beliefs about parenting in Argentinean, French, and American parents. Nevo and bin Khader (1995) investigated conceptions of an "intelligent child" in Chinese, Malay, and Indian mothers in Singapore. Fine, Voydanoff, and Donnelly (1994) compared beliefs about child well-being held by parents and stepparents. These studies and others (Harkness & Super, 1996a) report significant intercultural and intracultural differences in parental beliefs and suggest how these differences may influence developmental processes (Miller, 1995; Sigel, 1985).

Longitudinal researchers usually treat competence as a constellation of outcome variables, such as academic performance, conduct problems, and mental health (e.g., Garmezy, Masten, & Tellegen, 1984; Luthar, 1991; Waters & Sroufe, 1983). Defining competence, what it does and does not include, varies among studies, however. Synthesizing a definition from many studies, Masten and Coatsworth (1995) proposed that competence is "a pattern of effective performance in the environment, evaluated from the perspective of development in ecological and cultural context" (p. 724). Treating competence as evaluated performance, this definition is similar but not identical to anthropological use of the term. For many anthropologists, competence is thought of as the knowledge a culture member requires to act proficiently in his society. Keesing (1974) referred to it as the culture member's knowledge of expectations, ". . . his theory of what his fellows know, believe, and mean, his theory of the code being followed, the game being played, in the society into which he was born . . ." (p. 89).

Competence, viewed in these ways, reflects two traditional concerns in developmental psychology and sociocultural anthropology. As child development is the study of adaptation, psychologists examine the effectiveness of a child to adapt to a situation. For example, they may assess the effectiveness of a child in attracting his mother's attention away from a sibling. Behaviors are means to obtaining goals (establishing friendships, deceiving others, reducing anxiety) and there is variation in the child's success in achieving these goals. Rather than socializing agents, peers and parents, judging the effectiveness of a child's behavior, an outsider, the psychologist, views the child's performance steeped in theory and hypothesis. Anthropologists, in contrast, tend to be less concerned with effectiveness and more concerned with how people evaluate behavior in a particular setting in a particular society. What is culturally appropriate and inappropriate behavior? How do people label and explain behaviors of others? For anthropologists, the evaluation of behavior within the culture, the emic, is central to understanding developmental processes. Gilmore (1990), for example, adopted this perspective in describing what it is "to be a man" as well as "to make a man" in various societies. Given this dual nature of competence, effective performance and local evaluation, examining it requires contributions from both etically and emically inclined researchers, the psychologist and the anthropologist.

But why do we as developmentalists require better delineation of this evaluative part of competence, competence criteria? Describing competence criteria makes child development more globally relevant. Much of child development knowledge derives from studies of American and European children. Most the world's children, however, grow up under different conditions and, often, under different expectations. For example, in most regions of India, half of the girls do not complete primary school (UNICEF, 1995). Academic achievement for girls seems less a criterion of competence than performance of their chores (Rohner & Chaki-Sircar, 1988). Kagitçibasi (1995) described a Turkish preschool intervention where an outcome of the program, to promote independence in preschoolers, was not an outcome valued by many Turkish parents.

Given that criteria may vary across societies, how similar are criteria within a society, the United States, for example? In a provocative paper, Ogbu (1981) argued that competence criteria used in Black inner-city neighborhoods and White middle-class neighborhoods are distinct. These differences are so significant that standards assessing child competence, based on White middle-class children, may not be valid in assessing Black inner-city children. In making his case for distinct systems of competence in White middle-class and Black inner-city children, Ogbu discussed categories used by Black adolescents to describe behaviors and roles. Street smarts is an important criterion of competence in inner-city neighbor-

hoods. Similarly, Burton, Allison, and Obeidallah (1995) argued that African Americans in cities may use different criteria to assess outcome based
on a "revised" or restricted American dream. But do Black inner-city mothers and White mothers from middle-class neighborhoods use divergent
criteria? Studying several thousand Black, White, and Hispanic primary
school children in Chicago, Stevenson, Chen, and Uttal (1990) found that
Black and Hispanic mothers valued academic abilities in their children as
highly as White mothers. Although, Black inner-city and White suburban
parents may evaluate children in many of the same ways, it remains an
open question how similar are the criteria of parents and social workers.

The evaluation part of child competence, competence criteria, is the
focus of this chapter. Competence criteria are indicators that people in a
particular context use to decide that a child is "doing okay," that her
behavior meets the "specs" for her community. To be competent, the child
must conform to expectations of parents, peers, and others that she inter-
acts with daily. In an evolutionary approach to culture and development,
selection and competence criteria are usually parallel.

That parents and community members evaluate children's behavior
according to local standards is hardly controversial. Yet how this tendency
to evaluate emerged and its functions have received little attention. In the
following sections, I suggest that competence criteria in early childhood
emerged as a means to guide a parent's investment in an offspring. During
middle childhood, however, competence criteria become enmeshed with
competitive and cooperative interactions among families illustrated by my
fieldwork in the Eastern Caribbean.

COMPETENCE CRITERIA IN EARLY CHILDHOOD:
PARENTAL ESTIMATION OF CHILD PROSPECTS

Even early cultural relativists acknowledged that the proclivity of humans to
evaluate behavior is universal despite variation in criteria. "Courtesy, modesty, good manners, conformity to definite ethical standards are universal
but what constitutes courtesy, modesty, good manners, and ethical standards
are not universal," wrote the founder of American cultural relativism, Franz
Boas (Mead, 1961). Adults readily distinguish good and bad children
although attributes of good and bad children vary among cultures (Crystal
& Stevenson, 1995). The universality of evaluative systems suggests an
adaptive origin. A plausible scenario is that during hominid evolution the
ability to evaluate offspring coevolved with the increased dependence of
infants and competing demands of parents. According to parental investment theory (Draper & Harpending, 1987; Trivers, 1972), when resources
necessary to rear offspring become limited, parents become selective in the
care they "invest" in children. Parents invest in offspring most likely to survive

and reproduce. For offspring that are altricial and expensive to rear to maturity, the tendency to discriminate in investment should occur when offspring are quite young. For humans, then, forecasting children's future competence at an early age becomes critical when resources are scarce.

With the emergence of domestication, competence criteria probably become more selective rather than less. Archaeological and contemporary evidence indicates that the transition from a foraging to an agricultural way of life led to increasing occurrences of famines and epidemics (Cohen, 1986). Furthermore, breastfeeding duration became shorter. Contemporary hunter–gatherers who recently became agricultural breastfed almost a year less than those that remained hunter–gatherers. Agricultural mothers can rely on a grain gruel to wean their infants early (Lee, 1993). As breastfeeding declines, fecundity resumes, birth spacing becomes abbreviated and parental care more diluted. Thus, the emergence of domestication is often accompanied by a rise in infant deaths as well as births.

With this cultural transformation, parents face increased demands from their children for food as well as attention. When food and attention become limited, parents become discriminatory in the care they provide offspring. Food and attention became allocated based on the expectations about a child's chance to survive and succeed in the society. This hypothesis, that the tendency of parents to forecast future competence coemerged with domestication, has some partial support. Parents in foraging societies tend to be more affectionate toward children, whereas parents in agricultural societies tend to be less warm and more rejecting (Rohner, 1975).

How selective do parents become when they experience food scarcity? Two examples illustrate how parents in critical situations use infant attributes to forecast future competence of their children and how this forecasting becomes culturally justified.

De Vries (1987) examined infant mortality in the Masai of Kenya during famine. Among the Masai, birth spacing is short, 18 to 24 months, and mothers have, on average, six pregnancies. They are nomadic, depending greatly on their cattle that they herd over often arid areas. When drought occurs, cattle die, and the Masai are force to reduce their food intake.

Given this situation, De Vries examined infant survival during drought. In a small sample, he assessed infant and family characteristics before a drought and assessed mortality after. Factors such as socioeconomic conditions and maternal characteristics could not differentiate infants that survived from infants that perished. Surviving infants, however, tended to be temperamentally difficult and fussy according to the Thomas and Chess typology (an etic classification).

With the caveat of its small sample size, this study suggests that under certain conditions a "difficult" temperament becomes an asset rather than a liability. To account for this, De Vries proposed two processes. One process is that a fussy crying infant demands attention and may receive more breastfeeding to calm her than a more passive baby; the infant is like a "squeaky wheel" in need of oil and feeding may unintentionally reinforce the Masai infant to be "difficult." A second process is that the difficult Masai baby matches a cultural ideal. The Masai are warriors and favor assertiveness in children. In such a society, parents may consider a difficult baby a more promising one to invest in than a more quiet one. Both processes may influence parents tendency to favor the difficult infant over the easy one. Although emic-based research indicates that the Masai recognize personality as an evaluative dimension (Kirk & Burton, 1977), it still remains unclear whether selective care is an intentional process among the Masai.

A study of Brazilian slum dwellers provides another example of parental evaluation in a harsh environment. Scheper-Hughes (1987) interviewed mothers living in slums in Brazil, areas where water is dirty, food and medical care are scarce, and the under-five child mortality often approaches 40%. Breastfeeding is brief, believed to be of little use, and mothers have, on average, 10 pregnancies. Under these conditions, argued Scheper-Hughes, mother love becomes selective. Mothers often neglect infants and this neglect contributes to their death. Maternal investment greatly depends on the mother's perception of the infant's ability to survive and compete. Mothers prefer "fighters," active and precocious infants. She quotes one mother:

> I prefer a more active baby, because when they are quick and lively they will never be at a loss of life. The worst temperament in a baby is one that is dull and *morto de esprito* [lifeless], a baby so calm it just sits there without any energy. When they grow up they're good for nothing. (p. 194)

Although mothers may be initially reacting to temperamental cues they are also following a self-fulfilling prophecy. Even mild malnutrition pro-motes passivity in children (MacDonald, Sigman, Espinosa, & Neumann, 1994) and a passive infant may be vulnerable to what Scheper-Hughes called a "lethal form of negative feedback." A mother reduces feeding the baby who becomes even more malnourished and, hence, more passive until support is withdrawn and the infant dies.

These examples illustrate that under adverse conditions parents may appraise future competence of their infant using early appearing behavioral cues and following culture-based expectations. In the Masai competence forecasting these expectations reflect a *carpe-diem*-like world view valuing assertiveness and independence. In the Brazilian slums, expectations follow a similar world view called *luta*: life is a struggle. Some children win—they survive—while many lose. It is in these world views and unstable ecological settings, that competence forecasting and selective care during early child-hood becomes most apparent.

COMPETENCE CRITERIA IN MIDDLE CHILDHOOD: COMMUNITY RELATIONS

During middle childhood parents begin to evaluate a child's current competence, that is, her ability to perform effectively in developmentally critical tasks. Among !Kung hunter–gatherers, a child's entry into community responsibilities is gradual (Shostak, 1981). In contrast, in many agricultural societies, for example the Mixtecans of Mexico (Romney & Romney, 1963) and the Semai of Malaya (Dentan, 1979), when a child can talk, he becomes truly human, and is soon accorded chores and responsibilities. In agricultural societies, the end of infancy signals the beginning of a child's entry into the community. Their evaluation becomes based on their performance in their community. In the Six Cultures study (Whiting & Edwards, 1988), later expanded to include additional societies, all societies shared several general criteria in evaluating children. Children must show proper conduct toward adults, play well with peers, and proficiently perform chores. For example, older siblings often help take care of younger siblings (Weisner & Gallimore, 1977). However, societies differ in their reliance on these criteria. New England children had fewer chores than Gusii children of Kenya. Gusii parents, presumably, rank competence in chores higher than New England parents.

    In many societies, criteria during middle childhood reflect the concern of families to establish and maintain a positive reputation. In peasant societies, where interhousehold relations may be tense, family reputation often becomes a highly valued resource. Mockery, witchcraft accusations, and gossip are threats to reputation and may act to reduce family ambitions (Bailey, 1971). A child considered incompetent by adults in a community lowers not only his own life chances but tarnishes the reputation of his family. Thus, ensuring that one's children demonstrates competence in the community is part of maintaining family reputation. I illustrate this by presenting results from two studies in the Eastern Caribbean islands of Dominica and St. Vincent. A goal of these studies is to document developmental and cultural processes experienced by village children. After describing the context and methods, I discuss patterns in criteria as reflecting cultural processes in Caribbean villages.

COMPETENCE CRITERIA IN THE CARIBBEAN

> Wash the white clothes on Monday and put them on the stone heap; wash the color clothes on Tuesday and put them on the clothesline to dry; don't walk barehead in the hot sun; . . . soak salt fish overnight before you cook it; . . . always eat your food in such a way that it won't turn someone else's

stomach; on Sundays try to walk like a lady and not like the slut you are so bent on becoming. . . .

—Jamaica Kincaid (1985)

This passage from Jamaica Kincaid's short story "Girl" illustrates two aspects about parental evaluation of children in the rural Caribbean: concern with chores and the strong negativity or suspicion of parents. These and other aspects became clear to me during two field studies in Eastern Caribbean villages. Between 1988 and 1991, I spent 24 months living in a remote village on Dominica (Durbrow, 1993) and, between 1994 and 1996, I lived 9 months in a very similar village on St. Vincent. Both projects involved following schoolchildren over middle childhood to understand their adaptation to rapid community change. As my intent is to demonstrate connections between competence criteria and cultural processes, I briefly describe the context of these studies.

Dominica and St. Vincent have had similar histories (Honeychurch, 1984; Sutty, 1993). Both islands' indigenous populations resisted European colonization for a century and many natives today consider themselves descendants of the Caribs. By the 18th century, Europeans settled the islands brought in Africans as slaves to work plantation estates. Freed and escaped slaves, living in the rugged interior of Dominica, created Maroon communities or joined the Caribs in northern St. Vincent. With Emancipation in the mid-19th century, former slaves became estate workers and as the estates decline in the 20th century, became peasant farmers cultivating small holdings. Both islands became independent from the United Kingdom in the 1970s.

Dominicans and Vincentians differ most noticeably in language and religion. The French, who briefly controlled the island during the 18th century, deeply influenced Dominican culture. Although Dominicans speak a similar English dialect as Vincentians, they also speak a patois sometimes called Kwéyòl. Most Dominicans are Catholic, whereas most Vincentians are Protestants, although evangelical religions have gained converts in both islands. Obeah, a Caribbean form of magic (voodoo), appears to be more prevalent in Dominica than in St. Vincent.

The study communities are similar. Both are at the dead ends of rugged roads. Largely because of their remoteness, their development has been slower than other villages. Piped water, telephones, and electricity have only recently become available. In their economic development, the villages are almost a decade behind other villages although their modernization has accelerated lately.

Both villages have a traditional land use practice, sometimes called "family land." When the estates collapsed, the government deeded land to all villagers. Villagers have informally divided the land but no individual has title to it. Family land may contribute to distrust and competition in Caribbean villages when boundaries are unclear or when "outsiders" move into a village to settle (Layng, 1983). Although infrequent, disputes about land contribute to "vexation" or bad feelings among the villagers.

Distrust among families is more overt in the Dominican village than the Vincentian village. In contrast, the Vincentian villagers consider themselves friendly and "all one family" because of generations of intermarriage and few newcomers. Yet even in these "happy family" villages, discord occurs (Horowitz, 1967). For example, in the Vincentian village, many elders are uneasy about the Rastafarians or "bush men," Pentecostals and Baptists are mutually critical, and some parents feel that teachers set poor moral examples for children. During political campaigns, violence sometimes erupts.

In this situation, villagers try to minimize disparagement directed toward oneself and criticize others indirectly. This involves two cultural rules. The first is: One must not act "prideful," that is, one must not appear ambitious. The second rule is: One may make *cōmmess*, malicious gossip, but in a discrete manner. Gossipers should avoid referring to those being gossiped by name. One may say "the child of Mister over there" and nod toward a house. As many ethnographers of St. Vincent have noted (Abrahams, 1970; Katz, 1973; Morth, 1973; Rubenstein, 1987), this *cōmmess* is an important arena for social competition. I return to this by illustrating the entangling of these rules and competence criteria.

Caribbean family structure is variable, fluid, and complex (Clarke, 1966; Smith, 1962; Smith, 1988) although there are several broad patterns. In the villages I studied, approximately half the families are biparental. A couple may raise four or five children. Each mate often has children from previous relationships; children in one household often have different surnames. Fathers may live with their families year-round, especially if they are successful peasant farmers or fishermen. Alternatively, they may work most of the year overseas. Women typically have one or two children before they marry, if they marry at all.

Approximately half the families in the villages are nonnuclear; fathers do not live with or fully support their children. In these matrifocal and extended families, mothers, grandmothers, and aunts raise children. In many families, mothers may be largely absent, working in the larger towns as maids or sales clerks. In many families, grandmothers rear grandchildren while parents work in the cities or overseas. Grandfathers are usually too busy working in the fields to interact frequently with grandchildren. Thus even in these extended families, men usually stay on the periphery of child care.

Early childhood is a topsy-turvy time for Caribbean village children. Mothers, especially first-time mothers, indulge in their newborns. They dress them in their best clothes, buy a cap to cover their heads, and take them on visits to other households to proudly show them off. In this way, a young woman signals that she is fully an adult member of the village.

Older adults delight in playing with babies though some examine the babies for birth marks and features suggesting dubious paternity, a classic topic of *cōmmess*.

When infants enter their second or third years, mothers become less indulgent. As birth spacing is usually less than 3 years, it is around this time that many mothers become pregnant again. When a new child is born, mothers have much less time for their other children. As in other societies (Weisner & Gallimore, 1977), mothers often leave much of the care of toddlers to older siblings, especially girls. Older siblings escort, bathe, and dress younger siblings. They help prevent major mishaps: Even a lackadaisical boy grabs the hand of his small sister before a truck hurls by them on the village road. Nevertheless, accidents do occur (one child swallowed gasoline) and worm infestations, probably due to pica or eating contaminated foods, are common. In both villages, approximately one fourth of the children were mildly-to-moderately underweight in early childhood.

Older siblings also help socialize young children. They take them on play excursions where they meet other children and become acquainted with neighbors. They join neighborhood play groups and learn the names of village areas. They also acquire their play names such as, "Bishop" or "Woosh Woosh," nicknames that appear suddenly and last a lifetime.

During the transition to middle childhood, Caribbean children learn to perform chores. Mothers will send their 3 or 4 year olds with older children to the local shop. During these errands, they learn which shops to go to, what to buy, how much to pay, and how to greet the storekeeper. By age 5 or so, children learn to do these errands independently. Girls keep the household yard swept, wash dishes and clothes, help process coconuts, and admonish younger children to behave. Boys have slightly fewer chores. Their fathers, even if they do not live with them, may give them a goat or sheep to care for. Boys must move their animals daily to new pastures, tying them to a branch or some grass. Goats and sheep often become loose. A farmer can kill livestock found loose in his garden. By tending animals, children become aware of retribution.

When they are 5 years old, children attend the primary school in their village. At age 12 they take a national high school entrance examination. Those that pass may attend secondary school free although parents must make considerable efforts to find them lodging with appropriate supervision, textbooks, and clothes. Those that fail attend the village school for a few more years, then take the exam again. Most fail and leave school by age 15. The entrance examination has become the major rite of passage in the Eastern Caribbean and shapes a child's future. It rations the limited places in secondary schools (Payne & Barker, 1986). Most St. Vincent and Dominican children, especially village children, fail the examination (World Bank, 1993).

As unemployment in the East Caribbean is high, there are few opportunities for adolescents without a secondary education. Teenage boys who have finished village school spend most of their day playing and talking with other boys. They have few chores and adults disparagingly refer to them as "idling youths." Parents assign domestic chores to out of school teenage girls. More fortunate girls obtain a position in the towns, such as hotel maid. In contrast, youths with a secondary education, although not guaranteed a job, are more likely to get one.

Parents' Descriptions of Children

In these settings, what do Caribbean parents consider in evaluating competence in their children? As a first step, an assistant and I collected expressions parents use to refer to children. Asking parents to describe children is a sensitive subject as village children are often topics of *cōmmess.* Given this, we felt that brief and private interviewing was a better method to collect competence descriptors than focal group discussions. Although group discussions are attractive to researchers who spend little time in the field, they may miss important cultural variation in attitudes, especially in peasant villages where participants are reluctant to disclose opinions about the children of other families.

As part of a spot observation procedure, an assistant and I visited Dominican and Vincentian families several times weekly over months of fieldwork. Parents and caretakers (e.g., grandmothers, aunts) became accustomed to us. During these visits we asked parents to describe their child, someone else's child, or a particular behavior. When parents used a term describing a child we tried to clarify its use. For example, if a mother referred to her infant as "miserable" I asked her to specify in what situations the child was miserable.

Many of the descriptors of children used by Vincentians and Dominicans are listed in Table 5.1. Adults in both islands share many of the English dialect items but the Kwéyòl terms (spelled approximately) are exclusively used in Dominica. The meaning and context of commonly used terms are discussed next.

Troublesome. The most commonly used term to describe children is "troublesome" or, in Dominica, *a-bêtant.* Parents refer to preschool-age children as troublesome with a smile. Indeed, a small child is not likely to feel greatly reprimanded when a parent yells "Boy! You troublesome!" On the contrary, he may understand that he is considered cute. By age 4 or 5, troublesome becomes less an indulgent term and more an admonishment. Parents may call a 5-year-old troublesome when he argues with

TABLE 5.1
Parents' Descriptors of Child Behavior (Underlined Terms
in Dominican Kwéyòl and Spelled Approximately)

	Negativity	Common Example
A-betant / Troublesome	Mild	Failure to do chores
Ci-sep-til / Fussy	Mild	Does not eat
Coucha / Timid	Mild	Hides face from strangers
Miserable	Moderate	Does not attend to duties
Greedy	Moderate	Takes more than his share
Hardened	Moderate	Does not answer adults
Ka raisonné / Rude	Moderate	Talks back to adults
Lazy / Idle	Moderate	Does not attend to task
Evil or wicked	Moderate	Does not obey adults
Mal casé [badly broken]	Moderate	Mentally retarded
Mal lavé [badly raised]	Moderate	Rude to others

siblings or fails to go on an errand. For most villagers, almost all children are troublesome.

Hardened. A Vincentian mother of a 10-year-old son said of him: "He hardened"—he is stubborn. Little can be done to change the child. The mother, in using this term to describe her child, is also implying that she is not to blame because he is set in his ways.

Idling/Lazy. A middle-age man pointed to a 12-year-old boy, who recently failed the entrance examination, and told us "he lazy." All the boy does, the man complained, is "idling." This boy does not care for his goat, for example.

For younger children, *lazy* refers sometimes to a child's lack of application at school but more often to the child's reluctance to do chores. More often, lazy and idling describe adolescents who are no longer in school and who spend their day loitering in village common areas with their peers. *Lazy* reflects the tensions between the older and younger generations in the village. From the youth's perspective there is nothing to do in the village; no jobs and little entertainment. From the adult's perspective the adolescent is just an "idle youth" and living off his mother (Hourihan, 1973).

Parents' Descriptions of Competence

These terms, we soon found, described a "bad child" or an incompetent child rather than a competent one. To better capture what parents consider competence in children, we interviewed Vincentian parents in private semistructured interviews.

We interviewed 22 parents, 20 mothers and 2 fathers. Some women were grandmothers. All of them had some primary school education and about one third had some postprimary or secondary education. About one third were also relatively affluent: Their homes contained televisions and telephones.

The interview protocol, the Criteria of Child Competence Interview (CCC), was developed by Ann Masten and myself as part of a comparative study of parental evaluation in Turkey, Greece, Hong Kong, and the United States. The CCC is a semistructured protocol administered in face-to-face interviews with informants. The interviewer asks the parent to think of a child that is "doing well" or "doing okay" in the community. Parents should not imagine a perfect child, only a child in their community that they think is satisfactory. Parents do not identify children, only their gender and age. Once they have a competent child in mind they provide four ways in which the child was competent. Interviewers listed these descriptors verbatim and ask clarifying questions when descriptors were vague.

By the end of the interview, parents are asked to describe four types of children: girls ages 5–12 (preadolescent), boys ages 5–12 (preadolescent), girls ages 13–18 (adolescent), and boys ages 13–18 (adolescent). If informants are unable to describe competence for certain types of children, interviewers prompted once and left the response empty if needed. In the last CCC question, parents provide several reasons why some children "turn out okay while others do not."

We then extract descriptors of competence from the interviews and print them on cards. The six sorters, undergraduate students but of diverse nationalities,[2] sorted the items. Sorters place items into related groups, as many as they thought necessary. We assessed interagreement by computing intercorrelations among sorters. Agreement among sorters was high, ranging from .46 to .81. We then computed a cooccurrence matrix of sortings and factor analyzed the matrix (not the raw sortings) using Varimax rotation. Several findings emerged from analysis of interview data.

First, in the initial question, where we did not specify the child's gender, parents were unlikely to first think of adolescent boys as competent. Furthermore, respondents had much more difficulty thinking of competent adolescent boys than other types of children. These results suggest that models of adolescent boys are less salient in the village.[3]

---

[2]It is possible that our group of sorters organized items into different categories than Caribbean villagers would have. However, many hours of interviewing with Caribbean villagers about their attitudes toward children suggest to us that this is not likely.

[3]In a similar study of African American homeless families, Ann Masten and I found that parents had similar difficulty in identifying competent adolescent males. This is of little surprise as, in this setting, adolescent boys are at great risk of incarceration and death. As these youths face great challenges, models of competent adolescent boys may be rare.

TABLE 5.2
Parental Criteria of Child Competence. Proportion
of Total Items Mentioned by Respondents

	% Items
Respect and obedience to adults	31.7
Academically competent	22.1
Proficient with chores	12.0
Participates in activities	9.1
Sociable with peers	8.0
Regular church attendance	6.1
Good health and hygiene	4.2
Content nature	3.4
Miscellaneous	2.1
Stays at home	1.3

Second, factor analysis suggests that parents use many major and minor criteria in describing competent children listed in Table 5.2. Major factors were respect and obedience to adults, completing chores, doing well in school, getting on well with peers, and engaging in activities outside the home and school. Minor factors included attending church, good health habits, staying home, and having a content disposition. Despite its occurrence in the village, parents did not mention sibling care as an example of competence.

We then examined how parents apply these criteria of competence to different types of children. Figure 5.1 suggests that criteria are differentially applied to adolescent boys. Academic competence is less associated with adolescent boys. Instead, adolescent boys, more so than other children, are expected to be proficient in chores. As adults criticize adolescent boys

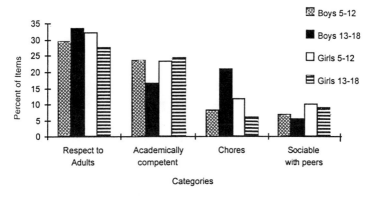

FIG. 5.1. Proportion of major criteria associated with different types of children.

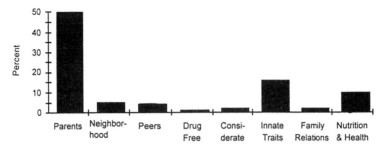

FIG. 5.2.   Reasons parents provide for the development of competence.

for being idle, the importance placed on chore performance accounts for adults' difficulty in identifying competent adolescent boys.

Lastly, what reasons did Vincentian village parents provide for the development of competence in children? As presented in Fig. 5.2, adequate parenting was most frequently mentioned as a key ingredient of competence. Competent children have firm and responsible caregivers. Paradoxically, the next most mentioned prerequisite for competence involved innate traits. Competent children are born intelligent ("it is in the blood" our respondents said) and are not "hardened."[4] This suggest that villagers recognize both the importance and the limits in parenting.

LINKS BETWEEN COMPETENCE CRITERIA
AND SOCIOCULTURAL PROCESSES

I suggested earlier that patterns in parental evaluation of children during middle childhood may reveal as much about sociocultural processes as they do about developmental processes. With the caveat that this research is still in its early stage, I describe how village parents' attitudes about children reflect increasing interhousehold tension, intergenerational conflict, and community modernization.

Child Manners and Interhousehold Relations

Interviews indicate that parents have strong concerns about the manners of their children. This concern is not new. Carlson (1973), who examined Vincentian dialect and manners two decades ago, writes:

> To behave "publicly" in St. Vincent, one must give evidence of his sense of propriety. It is "proper" to greet another with "good morning," "good afternoon," "good evening," or "good night," before continuing past him on the

---

[4]African American parents who are homeless considered safe neighborhoods an important necessity for the development of competence. Thus, ingredients of competence reflect beliefs about settings.

street. To fail to give this sort of greeting is to invite rebuke. . . . If a seven-year-old child going to Mr. Jones' shop for a half-pound of flour simply steps up to the counter and places the order, he may be refused service until he says, "Good evening, Mr. Jones." (p. 138)

Although this concern of public conduct seems to be disappearing, it is still important in the criteria of many adults, especially in the poorest and least educated. As the two villages become more populated and as villagers begin to gain title to their land, household relations are becoming less amicable. In ethnohistorical interviews, all respondents told me that relations between families were more cooperative a decade or more ago than now. *Koudmens* or cooperative work exchanges are becoming rare in farming. Factions have emerged: parents versus teachers, Christians versus Rastafarians. In this tense milieu, parents must take care that their children are not the source of "vexation" with their neighbors.

Yet, despite this emphasis on public manners, all parents I interviewed unanimously agreed that children are less well behaved today then 10 or more years ago. Furthermore, all adults believed that children have become less mannerly because of changes in punishment. When they were children it was permissible for any villager to punish a rude child, not just the child's parent. Teachers, following the British colonial tradition, flogged misbehaving children. If children complained about the punishment to their parents they could expect an even more severe beating.

Today, however, teachers are reluctant to punish children. They are afraid that the parents will retaliate by publicly cursing them. Likewise, adults such as shopkeepers rarely punish someone else's child. Why this change from community to parental discipline? One Vincentian man confided that "vexation," bad feelings, among neighbors has become more apparent over last the two decades. Children, he believes, recognize feuds between families and contribute to it by showing disrespect toward their family's antagonists. Parents and teachers understand that to punish children of others may lead to more vexation among families and are reluctant to do so. How interhousehold relations became so sensitive is not clear though it may be a consequence of decreasing availability of land and increasing homesteading of outsiders into the village. Whatever the historical processes, there is nearly unanimous agreement that the change in discipline has led to a generation of youths considered lazy, wicked, and worthless by many adults in the villages.

Pride

Almost all descriptors we collected were negative. Rarely do Dominicans describe children as *bwen lavé* (well brought up) and rarely do Vincentians refer to children as pleasant or well behaved. In home assessment interviews with Dominican and Vincentian parents, only a few admitted praising their child during the past week. This reticence to describe children or their behavior positively reflects a parent's theory of child development. Adults rarely praise children for fear that the they will become spoiled or that the child will become a "boaster." On the contrary, parents admonish, threaten, and occasionally beat their children for failure to obey. One special form of punishment is to force a child to kneel on a perforated coconut grater. The village theory of child development is that adults control children by negative not positive incentives. "Spare the cane, spoil the child." An implicit goal in this practice is to avoid rearing children that are "prideful" for showing pride invites criticism from others.

In this regard, community relations and child evaluation are entangled. Peasant communities often have processes inhibiting individual gains in status or wealth (Foster, 1974). In the Caribbean, one such process is gossip and reputation. Those who become ambitious jeopardize their reputations. In Dominica, villagers complain that when someone tries to improve his lot, perhaps by planting flowers or by buying a dress for her child, others will complain that the person is becoming greedy or has too much pride. Such criticism is sometimes called "petty jealousy."

To a slightly lesser extent this is true in the Vincentian village. Successful people, people who have a wage-paying job or who try to start village projects, risk criticism and sometimes hostility from others. For example, a successful young man complained that even people he has known all his life may verbally "knife him behind the back" at any moment. Abrahams (1970) explained that Vincentians fear *cōmmess* because they lose control of their names (reputation).

A child is not immune to this. Whereas a competent child is unlikely to be the target of *cōmmess*, a child deviating from the criteria becomes vulnerable. Making *cōmmess* about children, especially common among women (Abrahams, 1970), tarnishes the reputation of the child's family. In Dominica, to say that a child is *mal lavé*, badly raised, is to find fault more with the family than the child. Rivals in the villages may reduce each other's good name by criticizing children.

Success, then, is risky business in a Caribbean village. Children should be competent, they should not be foolish, but children who become prideful because they are praised or allowed to boast of their achievements become vulnerable to gossip and rebuke. Thus, to prevent this, parents refer to children, including often their own, negatively. In Caribbean villages, I have yet to read on a car bumper: "My child made the honor roll."

Adolescent Competence and Intergenerational Relations

Parental evaluations are most negative when Caribbean parents consider adolescents (Payne, 1993). Descriptors, "hardened," "wicked," suggest that the adolescent is a lost cause and that the parent washes her hands of him.

A child still in school, still preparing for the high school entrance examination, is rarely described so harshly. In contrast, boys in their mid teens who are out of school are considered already set in their ways. Paradoxically, their criticism may be one contributing factor, of many, that drives adolescent boys to becoming financial independent by cultivating marijuana.

Parents perception of teenage girls is different and their relationship is less laissez faire. Parents, particularly mothers, try to inhibit sexual liaisons of their daughters (Flinn, 1988; Smith, 1962). In the Dominican village, for example, a mother was said to have severely beaten her daughter for having premarital sex. When a girl becomes pregnant it is her parent, not the boy's, who will have to support the baby. Daughters may become pregnant while the mother is still of reproductive age, making the situation particularly acute. This concern about the sexuality of daughters is common and is a popular topic of *cōmmess.*

Change in Competence Criteria and Community Modernization

Ethnographic studies in development often give the impression that developmental processes are immune to social change. Competence criteria in these communities and other communities are rapidly changing. In Dominica, village schoolchildren are only occasionally reprimanded by an adult they pass by for failing to greet. In contrast to Carlson's (1973) observation, Vincentian village children on an errand to a shop are seldom refused service if they do not show proper deference to the shopkeeper and other adults. Adults still consider such children rude but as relations between families have become sensitive they withhold overt criticism.

At the moment, most adults evaluate children's competence by conduct to adults and performance in chores more so than by their competence in school. Why this is the case is not hard to identify. Most village children fail to pass the high school entrance examination. Many parents are resigned that their children will fail and that they have no hope in entering secondary school. Most do little to encourage academic competence. When a child brings home a bad report card, the parent often blames the child for being dull or, more likely, blames the teacher for being incompetent, uncaring, immoral, or nepotistic. Thus, most parents blame poor academic performance on external forces beyond their control; doing well academically is not among the highest priorities.

However, this is not true of all Dominican and Vincentian families we studied. Some families in the villages are affluent by rural standards. They live in large cinderblock houses, watch television, and own telephones. They enjoy a steady income from a wage-paying job or from an overseas working spouse. For these families, getting their child into secondary school is critical to maintaining the family reputation. Parents provide books and even spectacles for their children. Should their children fail the high school entrance examination, parents will go to considerable lengths to bypass the government education system and send their child to a school they must pay for. Because of their increasing status and affluence, they are aware that they are vulnerable to village *cōmmess*. Failure of their children to enter secondary school would embarrass most of these families.

The criteria of competence of these families differ in other ways. Completing chores are less important. Children may be excused from doing agricultural work or routine chores. Although parents demand that children obey them, proper respect to other adults is much less important than in families with traditional criteria. Parents in these families are also concerned about the company their children keep. They tend to know their children's playmates. They may discourage children from playing with children of families of poor reputation. Indeed, some families discourage their children from playing with other children outside school. Rather, they must stay home and only play with siblings.

Thus, presently, competence criteria are changing in the rural eastern Caribbean. In the traditional peasant-oriented system a competent child is a well-behaved child, a child that completes chores promptly and shows deference toward adults. As villages become less peasant-oriented and more economically developed, conduct toward all adults and ability to perform chores become less important than doing well in primary school and obtaining a secondary education.

CONCLUSIONS

This chapter has several aims. First, I proposed that inquiry into child competence can be mutually informative to the psychologist concerned about evaluating the effectiveness of performance (behavior) and the anthropologist concerned with how performance is evaluated in particular societies. Joint research in how parental criteria of competence influences children's development and how competence is evaluated within and across society helps to narrow the gap between developmental psychologists and emic-oriented researchers such as cultural psychologists. Competence can be a major knot tying together cultural and developmental processes.

Second, I suggested that the evaluative aspect of child competence, as reflected in competence criteria, originated as an adaptation to differentially allocate attention and resources based on a child's prospects. When resources are scarce, competence criteria during early childhood become most apparent. During middle childhood, competence criteria reflect sociocultural context, the expectations of community members, as illustrated by my fieldwork in two Eastern Caribbean villages. My aim was to show that gossip, reputation, intergenerational distrust, and community modernization are entangled in parents' evaluation of children.

Why are such studies of competence criteria worth the attention of anthropologists and psychologists? For anthropologists, competence criteria reveal the values and beliefs of people, how cultural processes interact with development, and how culture change is intertwined with developmental change. Examining competence criteria may reveal important within-cultural and intergenerational variation often neglected in ethnographies. For psychologists, given that many developmentalists acknowledge the influence of parental beliefs on developmental processes (e.g., Goodnow, 1996; Harkness & Super, 1996; Miller, 1995; Weisner, Matheson, & Bernheimer, 1996), it behooves them to place greater emphasis on delineating these beliefs. Furthermore, this effort would reveal the extent to which psychologists' conceptions of competence, evident in articles published in *Child Development* or *Developmental Psychology*, diverge from conceptions held by the people they study. In this regard, a critical question in child development becomes: Are local criteria of competence vastly different in populations discussed in these articles? If cultural processes in development are to become a cornerstone of child development inquiry, we need further studies comparing competence criteria, how these criteria shape development and link to larger processes such as cultural change. Psychologists sometimes assume a pattern is universal based on a small sample of highly industrialized populations (e.g., McCrae & Costa, 1997). It is especially important that we go beyond "journal-article populations" to examine how children are evaluated in developing communities—the majority of the world's children—where criteria of competence may be varied and undergoing the rapid transformation.

ACKNOWLEDGMENTS

I thank Ingrid Bozoky, Ann Masten, Mark Flinn, and the anonymous reviewer for their advice and help. Auke Tellegen provided generous assistance with the analysis. Ian William, Rolf Nelson, Derval Hayes, Megan Kirchner, Emily Jones, Holli Tonyan, and Wendy Woods also assisted. The Sigma Xi Foundation and the Fulbright Foundation supported Dominica fieldwork; Spencer Foundation and the Johann Jacobs Foundation funded St Vincent fieldwork. For their patience and kindness, *méci* and many thanks to the peoples of Dominica and St. Vincent.

REFERENCES

Abrahams, R. D. (1970). A performance-centered approach to gossip. *Man, 5,* 290–301.
Bailey, F. G. (1971). *Gifts and poison.* Oxford: Basil Blackwell & Mott.
Bornstein, M., Tamis-LeMonda, C. S., Pascual, L., Haynes, M., Painter, K. M., Galperín, C. Z., & Pêcheux, M. G. (1996). Ideas about parenting in Argentina, France, and the United States. *International Journal of Behavioral Development, 19*(2), 347–367.

Burton, L. M., Allison, K. W., & Obeidallah, D. (1995). Social context and adolescence: Perspectives on development among inner-city African-American teens. In L. J. Crockett & A. C. Crouter (Eds.), *Pathways through adolescence: Individual development in relation to social context* (pp. 119–138). Hillsdale, NJ: Lawrence Erlbaum Associates.

Carlson, P. E. (1973). Cognition and social function in the West Indian dialect: Stubbs. In T. M. Fraser (Ed.), *Windward road: Contributions to the anthropology of St. Vincent* (Vol. 12, pp. 123–147). Amherst: University of Massachusetts.

Chagnon, N. A. (1983). *Yąnomamö: The fierce people* (3rd ed.). New York: Holt, Rinehart & Winston.

Chisholm, J. S. (1993). Death, hope, and sex: Life-history theory and the development of reproductive strategies. *Current Anthropology, 34*(1), 1–24.

Clarke, E. (1966). *My mother who fathered me: A study of the family in three selected communities in Jamaica* (2nd ed.). London: George Allen & Unwin.

Cohen, M. (1986). The significance of long term changes in human diet and food economy. In M. Harris & E. Ross (Eds.), *Food and evolution: Towards a theory of human food habits* (pp. 261–283). Philadelphia: Temple University Press.

Crystal, D. S., & Stevenson, H. W. (1995). What is a bad kid? Answers of adolescents and their mothers in three cultures. *Journal of Research on Adolescence, 5*(1), 71–91.

De Vries, M. W. (1987). Cry babies, culture, and catastrophe: Infant temperament among the Masai. In N. Scheper-Hughes (Ed.), *Child survival.* Boston: D. Reidel.

Dentan, R. K. (1979). *The Semai: A nonviolent people of Malaya.* New York: Harcourt Brace College Publishers.

Draper, P., & Harpending, H. (1987). Parent investment and the child's environment. In J. Lancaster, J. Altmann, A. Rossi, & L. Sherrod (Eds.), *Parenting across the lifespan: Biosocial dimensions* (pp. 207–235). New York: Aldine deGruyter.

Durbrow, E. (1993). *School performance and behavior problems of Caribbean children: Association with pediatric risk and growth, home conditions, and temperament.* Unpublished doctoral dissertation, University of Missouri, Columbia, MI.

Fine, M., Voydanoff, P., & Donnelly, B. W. (1994). Parental perceptions of child well-being: Relations to family structure, parental depression, and marital satisfaction. *Journal of Applied Developmental Psychology, 15*(2), 165–186.

Flinn, M. V. (1988). Parent-offspring interactions in a Caribbean village: Daughter guarding. In M. M. L. Betzig & P. Turke (Eds.), *Human reproductive behavior.* London: Cambridge University Press.

Foster, G. M. (1974). Limited good or limited goods: Observations on Acheson. *American Anthropologist, 76,* 53–57.

Garmezy, N., Masten, A. S., & Tellegen, A. (1984). The study of stress and competence in children: A building block for developmental psychopathology. *Child Development, 55*(1), 97–111.

Gilmore, D. D. (1990). *Mankind in the making: Cultural concepts in masculinity.* New Haven, CT: Yale University Press.

Goodnow, J. J. (1996). From household practices to parents' ideas about work and interpersonal relationships. In S. Harkness & C. Super (Eds.), *Parents' cultural belief systems: Their origins, expressions, and consequences* (pp. 313–344). New York: Guilford Press.

Harkness, S., & Super, C. (Eds.). (1996a). *Parents' cultural belief systems: Their origins, expressions, and consequences.* New York: Guilford Press.

Harkness, S., & Super, C. (1996b). Introduction. In S. Harkness & C. Super (Eds.), *Parents' cultural belief systems: Their origins, expressions, and consequences* (pp. 1–23). New York: Guilford Press.

Honeychurch, L. (1984). *The Dominica story: A history of the island.* Dominica, West Indies: The Dominica Institute.

Horowitz, M. M. (1967). *Morne-Paysan: Peasant village in Martinique.* New York: Holt, Rinehart & Winston.

Hourihan, J. J. (1973). Youth employment: Stubbs. In T. M. Fraser (Ed.), *Windward road: Contributions to the anthropology of St. Vincent.* Amherst: University of Massachusetts.

Kagitçibasi, Ç. (1995). Is psychology relevant to global human development issues? Experience from Turkey. *American Psychologist, 50*(4), 293–300.

Katz, P. S. (1973). Some aspects of gossip: Villo point. In T. M. Fraser (Ed.), *Windward Road: Contributions to the anthropology of St. Vincent* (pp. 80–89). Amherst: Department of Anthropology, University of Massachusetts.

Keesing, R. M. (1974). Theories of culture. *Annual Review of Anthropology, 3,* 73–97.

Kincaid, J. (1985). *At the bottom of the river.* New York: Adventura.

Kirk, L., & Burton, M. (1977). Meaning and context: A study of contextual shifts in meaning of Maasai personality descriptors. *American Ethnologist, 4*(4), 734–761.

Layng, A. (1983). *The Carib reserve: Identity and security in the West Indies.* New York: University Press of America.

Lee, R. B. (1993). *The Dobe Ju/'hoansi* (2nd ed.). New York: Harcourt Brace College Publishers.

Luthar, S. (1991). Vulnerability and resiliency: A study of high-risk adolescents. *Child Development, 62,* 600–616.

MacDonald, M. A., Sigman, M., Espinosa, M. P., & Neumann, C. G. (1994). Impact of a temporary food shortage on children and their mothers. *Child Development, 65,* 404–415.

Masten, A. S. (1989). Resilience in development: Implications of the study of successful adaptation for developmental psychopathology. In D. Cicchetti (Ed.), *The emergence of a discipline: Rochester symposium on developmental psychopathology* (Vol. 1, pp. 261–294). Hillsdale, NJ: Lawrence Erlbaum Associates.

Masten, A., & Coatsworth, D. (1995). Competence, resilience, and psychopathology. In D. Cicchetti & D. J. Cohen (Eds.), *Developmental psychopathology, Vol. 2: Risk, disorder, and adaptation* (pp. 715–752). New York: Wiley.

McCrae, R. R., & Costa, P. T. (1997). Personality trait structure as a human universal. *American Psychologist, 52*(5), 509–516.

Mead, M. (1961). *Coming of age in Samoa.* New York: Morrow Quill Paperbacks.

Miller, S. A. (1995). Parents' attributions for their children's behavior. *Child Development, 66,* 1557–1584.

Morth, G. E. (1973). Commess: Traditional and official forms of social control. In T. M. Fraser (Ed.), *Windward Road: Contributions to the anthropology of St. Vincent* (pp. 73–79). Amherst: Department of Anthropology, University of Massachusetts.

Nevo, B., & bin Khader, A. (1995). Cross-cultural, gender, and age differences in Singaporean mothers' conceptions of children intelligence. *Journal of Social Psychology, 135,* 509–517.

Ogbu, J. (1981). The origins of human competence: A cultural ecological perspective. *Child Development, 52,* 413–429.

Payne, M. A. (1993). Barbadian adolescents in 1991: Adult perceptions of change over a decade. *International Journal of Adolescence and Youth, 4*(2), 143–156.

Payne, M. A., & Barker, D. O. (1986). Still preparing children for the 11+: Perceptions of parental behaviour in the West Indies. *Educational Studies, 12*(3), 313–325.

Rogoff, B., & Morelli, G. (1989). Perspectives on children's development from cultural psychology. *American Psychologist, 44*(2), 343–348.

Rohner, R. P. (1975). *They love me, they love me not: A worldwide study of the effects of parental acceptance and rejection.* New Haven, CT: Human Relations Area Files Press.

Rohner, R., & Chaki-Sircar, M. (1988). *Women and children in a Bengali village.* Hanover, NH: University Press of New England.

Romney, K., & Romney, R. (1963). The Mixtecans of Juxtlahua, Mexico. In B. Whiting (Ed.), *Six cultures: Studies of child rearing* (pp. 541–692). New York: Wiley.

Rubenstein, H. (1987). *Coping with poverty: Adaptive strategies in a Caribbean village.* London: Westview Press.

Rutter, M., & Quinton, D. (1984). Long-term follow-up of women institutionalized in childhood: Factors promoting good functioning in adult life. *British Journal of Developmental Psychology, 18,* 225–234.

Sameroff, A. J., & Seifer, R. (1990). Early contributors to developmental risk. In J. Rolf, A. S. Masten, D. Cicchetti, K. H. Nuechterlein, & S. Weintraub (Eds.), *Risk and protective factors in developmental psychopathology.* New York: Cambridge University Press.

Saxe, G. B. (1991). *Culture and cognitive development: Studies in mathematical understanding.* Hillsdale, NJ: Lawrence Erlbaum Associates.

Scheper-Hughes, N. (1987). Culture, scarcity, and maternal thinking: Mother love and child death in Northeast Brazil. In N. Scheper-Hughes (Ed.), *Child survival* (pp. 187–208). Boston: D. Reidel.

Schwartz, T. (1992). Anthropology and psychology: An unrequited relationship. In T. Schwartz, G. M. White, & C. A. Lutz (Eds.), *New directions in psychological anthropology* (pp. 324–349). New York: Cambridge University Press.

Shostak, M. (1981). *Nisa: The life and words of a !Kung woman.* New York: Vintage.

Shwalb, B. J., Shwalb, D. W., & Shoji, J. (1994). Structure and dimensions of maternal perceptions of Japanese infant temperament. *Developmental Psychology, 30*(2), 131–141.

Shweder, R. A. (1990). Cultural psychology—What is it? In J. W. Stigler, R. A. Shweder, & G. Herdt (Eds.), *Cultural psychology: Essays on comparative human development* (pp. 1–43). New York: Cambridge University Press.

Shweder, R. A. (1991). *Thinking through cultures: Expeditions in cultural psychology.* Cambridge, MA: Harvard University Press.

Sigel, I. E. (Ed.). (1985). *Parental belief systems: The psychological consequences for children.* Hillsdale, NJ: Lawrence Erlbaum Associates.

Silva, P. A. (1990). The Dunedin Multidisciplinary Health and Development Study: A 15 year longitudinal study. *Paediatric & Perinatal Epidemiology, 4*(1), 76–107.

Smith, M. G. (1962). *Kinship and community in Carriacou.* New Haven, CT: Yale University Press.

Smith, R. T. (1988). *Kinship and class in the West Indies: A genealogical study of Jamaica and Guyana.* Cambridge, England: Cambridge University Press.

Spiro, M. E. (1984). Some reflections on cultural determinism and relativism with special reference to emotion and reason. In R. Shweder & R. A. LeVine (Eds.), *Culture theory: Essays on mind, self, and emotion* (pp. 323–346). New York: Cambridge University Press.

Stevenson, H. W., Chen, C., & Uttal, D. H. (1990). Beliefs and achievement: A study of black, white, and hispanic children. *Child Development, 61,* 508–523.

Sutty, L. (1993). *St Vincent and the Grenadines.* London: Macmillan.

Trivers, R. L. (1972). Parental investment and sexual selection. In B. Campbell (Ed.), *Sex selection and the descent of man.* Chicago: Aldine deGruyter.

UNICEF. (1995). *The state of the world's children 1995.* Oxford: Oxford University Press.

Waters, E., & Sroufe, L. A. (1983). Social competence as a developmental construct. *Developmental Review, 3,* 79–97.

Weisner, T., Matheson, C. C., & Bernheimer, L. P. (1996). American cultural models of early influence and parent recognition of developmental delays: Is earlier always better than later? In S. Harkness & C. Super (Eds.), *Parents' cultural belief systems: Their origins, expressions, and consequences* (pp. 496–531). New York: Guilford Press.

Weisner, T., & Gallimore, R. (1977). My brother's keeper: Child and sibling caretaking. *Current Anthropology, 18*(2), 169–190.

Werner, E. E., & Smith, R. S. (1989). *Vulnerable but invincible: A longitudinal study of resilient children and youth.* New York: Adams, Bannister, Cox.

Whiting, B., & Edwards, C. (1988). *Children of different worlds: The formation of social behavior.* Cambridge, MA: Harvard University Press.

World Bank. (1993). *Caribbean region: Access, quality, and efficiency in education.* Washington, DC: World Bank.

Worthman, C. M. (1992). Cupid and psyche: Investigative syncretism in biological and psychological anthropology. In T. Schwartz, G. M. White, & C. A. Lutz (Eds.), *New directions in psychological anthropology* (pp. 150–178). Cambridge, England: Cambridge University Press.

Yang, B., Ollendick, T. H., Dong, Q., Xia, Y., & Lin, L. (1995). Only children and children with sibling in the People's Republic of China: Levels of fear, anxiety, and depression. *Child Development, 66,* 1301–1311.

Chapter 6

Cultural Influences in a Multicultural Society: Conceptual and Methodological Issues

Vonnie C. McLoyd
University of Michigan

As we stand at the threshold to the 21st century, never has it been more important that we gain improved understanding of cultural influences on children's development and carefully attend to the implications of these influences for policy and practice. This imperative derives from a confluence of factors, among them: (a) the increasing heterogeneity of the American population with respect to its racial and ethnic composition and relatedly, the growing importance of the productivity of racial and ethnic minorities to the economic and social well-being of American society; (b) the strong racial and ethnic cleavages in housing patterns, schooling, and myriad aspects of social life in American society that mitigate against cultural homogenization; and (c) the linkages among race, ethnicity, and culture. The past decade ushered in increases in the proportion of racial and ethnic minorities in the American population that were more dramatic than at any time in the 20th century. These increases were especially marked in the child and adolescent population. For example, in 1980, of all American children between the ages of 10 and 19, 75.8% were non-Latino Whites, 14.2% were African Americans, 7.8% were Latinos, 1.5% were Asian/Pacific Islanders, and 0.8% were American Indians. By 1992, the comparable figures were 68.8%, 14.8%, 12.1%, 3.4%, and 1%, respectively. The trend toward increasing racial and ethnic diversity in the American population is projected to continue for several decades (U.S. Bureau of the Census, 1994).

These recent and projected increases in the proportion of racial and ethnic minorities in the American population are driven primarily by two factors: (a) higher immigration rates of minorities, compared to immigration rates of non-Latino Whites of European or Middle Eastern descent, and (b) slightly higher fertility rates of immigrants, compared to native-born Americans (Martin & Midgley, 1994). Whereas most immigrants who came to America prior to the late 1950s were from northern and western European countries, by the 1980s, 85% of all immigrants arriving in the United States were from Latin American and Asian countries, whereas only 10% were from Europe. Mexico, the Philippines, Vietnam, China, and Korea, respectively, were the top five countries of origin. Caribbean countries, taken together, were the second largest source of immigrants during the 1980s (following Mexico), most of whom were from the Dominican Republic (28%), followed by Jamaica (24%), Cuba (18%), Haiti (16%), and Trinidad and Tobago (4% combined; U.S. Bureau of the Census, 1994). A significant proportion of today's immigrants have skin color of a darker hue (e.g., Dominicans, Haitians, Mexicans), and consequently, bear a stigma not experienced by European immigrants and their descendants. Immigrants of previous eras confronted dilemmas born of conflicting cultures, but they had the advantage of being uniformly White (Portes & Zhou, 1993).

The shift in the race and ethnicity of American immigrants occurred principally in response to the Immigrant Act of 1965 that instituted change from a geography-based to a familial- and skill-based preference system for selecting immigrants. Subsequent immigration reforms during the 1980s legalized significant numbers of undocumented workers (and their families) and made it even easier to bring skilled immigrants into the United States (Martin & Midgley, 1994). Underlying the latter reforms were demands for cheap labor, especially in the agricultural sector, and growing fear by employers that actual and anticipated shortages of skilled workers would ultimately undermine American competitiveness in the global economy (Martin, 1994).

Increases in the proportion of racial and ethnic minorities in the American population are occurring in the context of declines in the proportion of adolescents and young adults in the total American population. Between 1980 and 1992, the proportion of 10 to 19 year olds in the American population dropped from 17.4% to 13.8% (U.S. Bureau of the Census, 1994). This decline, first discernible in the early 1980s, is largely a function of low birth rates and the huge generation that preceded the current cohort of American youth, commonly known as the baby boomers. Born during the high-fertility years from 1945 to 1964, this generation is nearly 50% larger than that born between 1925 and 1944, and is 11% larger than the succeeding generation born between 1965 and 1984. The proportion of adolescents and young adults in the American population is not expected to grow substantially during the next two decades because birth rates have remained low during the 1980s and 1990s and because Americans' preference for small families is unlikely to wane (U.S. Bureau of the Census, 1994; Wetzel, 1987). A major consequence of the decline in the proportion of adolescents and young adults is that the number of entrants into the labor force will decrease and the ratio of workers to retirees will shrink. In effect, increases in the minority segment of the population mean that as non-Hispanic Whites age, they will be increasingly dependent on the productivity of African American, Latino, and Asian workers. The economic and social well-being of the nation, then, will depend even more than at present on its ability to enhance the intellectual and social skills of all its youth (Edelman, 1987). These demographic trends demand increased understanding of the pathways to successful and problematic development in ethnic and racial minority children and the contribution of cultural processes to these outcomes (McLoyd, 1998).

In addition to the demographic trends outlined earlier, it is arguable that culture constitutes a potentially potent influence on children's development precisely because of the presence of multiple factors within American society that mitigate against cultural homogenization. Not the least of these is widespread, entrenched racial and ethnic segregation in housing, schooling, and social relations (Hacker, 1992). In addition, the youth of today's immigrants are notably less likely than their counterparts in the early 20th century to believe that rejection of the values and folkways of their parents' homeland is a prerequisite to success in American society. Many espouse economic, but not cultural, assimilation into mainstream society. Furthermore, today's immigrants are most likely to settle in inner-city neighborhoods, where assimilation often means joining a world that is antagonistic to the American mainstream because of its collective experience of racism and economic exploitation (Portes & Zhou, 1994; Sontag, 1993).

The challenges involved in illuminating the role of culture in child development are as formidable as the imperatives are great. Although culture and its relation to development have been a focus of concern for several decades among anthropologists, leading journals in child and adolescent development continue to show a conspicuous paucity of research in this area. This is no doubt due to many factors, but one in particular stands out as both fundamentally important and eminently remediable: Researchers who potentially might be interested in studying the interplay between culture and development have neither had the training nor research instruments needed to undertake high-quality programs of research on the topic.

The notion of culture as a complex social context that impinges on development is given short shrift in core human development courses, no doubt one of the legacies of a discipline whose core objective in its early beginnings was to identify and trace the development of universal cognitive and social processes. As a result, for too many of us in the field, the concept of culture continues to evoke apprehension and trepidation, on the one hand, and overly simplistic and dubious notions on the other. In addition, training in this field typically provides neither instruction about research methods common in anthropology and characteristic of the emic approach, nor experiences that permit students to acquire and practice the skills needed to gather broad knowledge about ostensibly different cultural groups. Given the extensive racial and ethnic segregation in housing, schooling, and social relations that exists in the United States (Hacker, 1992; e.g., two thirds of non-Hispanic Whites currently live in neighborhoods that are at least 90% White; Edmondson, 1994), and the resulting ignorance about individuals from different racial and ethnic backgrounds, the need for such instruction is no less critical in advancing our understanding of subcultural influences within the American population as for studying transnational differences.

A controversial new field of academic research labeled "whiteness studies" may spur scholarly interest in cultural processes in children's development. This emergent area of study, itself a product of Whites' recognition that they are members of an increasingly multiracial and multicultural society, is predicated on the view that whites need to recognize themselves as a racial group in order to understand their history of privilege and to deal more equitably with other racial groups. Proponents tout such recognition as a needed antidote to Whites' perception of themselves and their culture as a raceless norm, arguing that it will enhance, rather than undermine, racial harmony, as long as Whites "also accept that they are not better biologically than others, or the standard-bearers of official American culture" (Yemma, 1997, p. G3). Critics, on the other hand, caution that conceding validity to whiteness as a category perpetuates injustice and furthers White-identity racism. Obviously, it will be years before we can judge the relative merits of these competing claims. The point to be made here is that this movement may be a harbinger of increasing attention to cultural processes in development and human behavior, for better or worse. In the sections that follow, I discuss some of the conceptual and methodological challenges that arise in the pursuit of these issues, bringing in some of the research described in this volume for illustrative purposes. I focus specifically on the study of cultural processes and child development within American borders, but obviously many of the same issues arise when the context is transnational.

DEFINING AND DIMENSIONING CULTURE

Defining culture is fundamental to the study of cultural influences on children's development, although a universally accepted definition of culture has proven elusive. As Guerra and Jagers (1998) observe:

There is considerable disagreement among scholars as to the precise meaning of the term [culture]. In its broadest sense, culture refers to a way of
life of a social group that includes shared norms, beliefs, values, and language, as well as shared organizations and institutions. . . . Clearly, culture
is not a unitary phenomenon, but rather a highly complex social context.
. . . Perhaps the most relevant feature of culture is its role in determining
the framework individuals use for making sense of the world—what could
be viewed as the social-cognitive component of culture. . . . This meaning
goes beyond language and symbols, and provides individuals with a template
for organizing social experience, although individuals within a given culture
still vary greatly in terms of how they interpret and understand their social
world. Such a template includes implicit norms regarding appropriate feelings and behaviors in specific situations, often referred to as the subjective
culture of the group, . . . as well as particular values and worldviews, also
referred to as the fundamental culture of the group.

The chapters in this volume reflect the wide-ranging conceptions, levels,
and elements of culture referred to by Guerra and Jagers (1998). Heath
(chap. 3, this volume), for example, focuses on language as an instrument
of enculturation of the norms of mainstream work environments,
demonstrating how shifting roles and demands of specific tasks performed
under adult supervision within youth organizations provoke substantive
changes in youth's linguistic practices and acquisition of specific syntactic
and discourse forms. Burton and Price-Spratlen (chap. 4, this volume), on
the other hand, direct their attention to neighborhood culture as
perceived, transmitted, and influenced by children. They argue com-
pellingly that development of conceptual and methodological approaches
that incorporate the definitions and meanings children accord to their
neighborhoods will forge advances in our understanding of the impact of
neighborhoods on children's development. Culture as conceived by
Durbrow (chap. 5, this volume), in his study of linkages between social
relations and criteria of childhood competence is broader still, encompassing language, religion, interhousehold relations, economic development,
land-use policy, and childrearing values and practices, among other things.
Notwithstanding these vast differences, each program of research detailed by the contributors to this volume affirms the basic notion of culture
as a highly complex, multidimensional social context, rather than as a
monolithic, nominal variable. What guideposts, then, does one use to
dissect cultural context into those dimensions or facets most critical to
understanding the domain of child functioning at issue? This challenge is
not unlike that involved in understanding the influence on human behavior of social class, which like culture, is a contextual variable comprised
of multiple components or dimensions. Addressing himself to the latter
issue, House (1981) has argued persuasively that tracing the processes
through which social structures, positions, or systems affect the individual

involves three theoretical tasks. First, we must understand the multiple aspects, dimensions, and components of the social structure, position, or system in question, and ultimately, develop conceptual frameworks that specify which of these are most relevant to understanding the outcomes of interest. Second, on the grounds that social structures, positions, or systems influence individuals through their effects on social interactional patterns, stimuli, and events that individuals experience in their daily lives, House maintains that we must understand the proximate social stimuli and interpersonal interactions associated with social class that impinge directly on the individual. Finally, we need to understand when, how, and to what extent these proximate experiences affect behavior, a task that requires documenting the psychological processes through which interactions and stimuli are perceived, processed, and accommodated.

The research presented in this volume addresses to varying degrees these theoretical tasks as applied to culture. Cooper's (chap. 2, this volume) window to culture brings into focus four constituents: (a) everyday routines or activity settings, (b) central socialization figures, (c) patterns of communication or cultural scripts, and (d) familial values, goals, and aspirations. They represent Cooper's appraisal of how best to "unpackage" culture to understand identity development and academic achievement in adolescents. Identified in the ecocultural framework articulated by Weisner and his colleagues (Weisner, Gallimore, & Jordan, 1988) as processes and mechanisms through which the child becomes a cultural being, these dimensions appear to be universally applicable, although obviously their manifestations will differ among cultures.

Although not explicitly enumerated, similar dimensions (e.g., cultural scripts; familial values, goals, and aspirations) emerged in Durbrow's intriguing study of the linkages between social relations and the criteria of competence for children in two rural, Eastern Caribbean villages, Dominica and St. Vincent. According to Durbrow, one competes in Caribbean villages not by maximizing prestige but by minimizing disparagement directed toward oneself and attacking one's enemies. This rule governing social stratification finds expression in two cultural scripts: (a) a proscription against acting "prideful" or appearing ambitious, and (b) acceptance of the practice of spreading malicious gossip about rivals (cõmmess). Durbrow looked for and found displays of these scripts in the criteria for childhood competence, lending support to the view that the indicators that people use to decide that a child is "okay" are indicative of key cultural values and beliefs. Children in these two communities were deemed as competent by adults if they were self-effacing, achieved at levels below the threshold that invites mockery, rebuke, or gossip; completed domestic chores promptly; showed respect and deference toward adults; and maintained positive relations with peers. Preservation of the reputation or good name of the child's family depended on the child's display of these behaviors. Evidence of the cultural scripts also were found in parental behavior toward and perception of children. Few parents, for example, described their children positively or admitted to praising their children for fear that the child would become prideful and evoke criticism from others. Durbrow also detected changes in competence criteria and developmental experiences traceable to economic, and ultimately, cultural change. In particular, he found evidence that as the availability of wage-paying jobs (as alternatives to farm labor) increased, maintaining the family reputation increasingly depended on getting the child into secondary school. This, in turn, lessened the tendency to evaluate children's competence in terms of completion of domestic chores, respect and deference toward adults, and positive peer relations, and conversely, increased the salience of academic performance and obedience toward parents (as opposed to all adults) as competence criteria. As these investigations demonstrate, illumination of the role of culture requires the unpackaging of culture, a conceptual task that should be guided by some understanding of the pertinent dimensions of culture most relevant to the developmental outcomes of interest.

ASCERTAINING THE INDIVIDUAL'S CULTURAL FRAMEWORK

Assuming that cultural identity is a critical mediator of cultural influences on behavior, efforts to illuminate the role of culture in children's development should be greatly enhanced by an understanding of the individual's cultural framework. Depending on the research, it may be the parent (i.e., in the role of socialization agent), the child (i.e., as an active decision maker who selects from an array of possible contexts and circumstances), or some other individual whose cultural framework is most critical. This task is relatively easy in cross-cultural research in which individuals from readily identifiable, relatively homogeneous cultural groups are contrasted with each other or with White middle-class Americans. However, making this determination is markedly more difficult when the research focuses exclusively on individuals who live in a culturally diverse society such as the United States where "individuals belong to a multiplicity of overlapping social groups, including groups defined by race, gender age, religion, social class, language, immigrant status, minority status, and ethnic identification" (Guerra & Jagers, 1998).

In contemporary developmental research focused on the American population, race and ethnicity are commonly used as markers of culture. Although a large number of ethnic groups exist within the White non-Latino segment of the American population (e.g., Italians, Jews), researchers interested in the influence of culture within the American context most often have focused on individuals belonging to ethnic minority groups, typically African Americans and Latinos. The customary use of racial and ethnic minority status as proxies of culture, driven in large measure by convenience, is not without justification, given the potent commonality of experience associated with minority status (i.e., racism, oppression, economic disadvantage, segregation from mainstream social institutions) and the fact that these groups have distinctive behaviors and institutions that can be viewed as artifacts of culture (e.g., language, religious institutions and practices). Nonetheless, as others have argued, this practice is problematic on several counts and consequently should be viewed, at best, only as a preliminary step in evaluating an individuals' cultural framework or experience.

First, membership in an ethnic or racial minority group is not equivalent to a common cultural experience for individuals given the wide variation that exists within these groups in terms of ethnic identity, social class, regional identification (e.g., Southerners vs. Northerners) and, among Latinos, in terms of country of origin, generational history or recency of immigration, acculturation status, language preference, and numerous other dimensions. Further, it is dubious to assume that the historical experience of one's ancestors is the primary determinant of one's cultural framework. A less salient, but nevertheless notable limitation of classification schemes based on racial and ethnic minority status is their inherent exclusion of racially or ethnically mixed children or adopted children who are ethnically or racially different from their adoptive parents (Guerra & Jagers, 1998; Weisner et al., 1988). We must move beyond this spurious cultural classification system and rely more on categorization systems based on individuals' experiences and perspectives. Dimensions of culture of the kind used in Cooper's research to dissect cultural context may also hold promise as a strategy to categorize individuals in terms of their cultural experience and cultural framework (e.g., knowledge, endorsement, and enactment of groups' cultural scripts; display of behaviors consistent with groups' distinctive norms and values). Ultimately, the level of specification of a respondent's cultural framework warranted will depend on the nature of the research questions, though any classification system that is reliable and based on how individuals interpret and understand their social world is likely to be superior to one based on ethnic or racial group membership.

Judging the Validity of Research on Cultural Processes

Research on cultural processes in child development that involves comparison of social or cultural groups should be subjected to evaluative standards beyond those typically used to judge the adequacy of research on child development generally. Some of the more important of these standards center around cultural and interpretative validity.

Cultural Validity. How well one conceptualizes and operationalizes dimensions of culture (e.g., cultural scripts, familial values) characteristic of a particular cultural group is a crucial criteria for judging the external validity of research on cultural processes. Current approaches to the conceptualization of external validity emphasize population, ecological, and construct validity. However, a more adequate assessment of the validity of comparative research involving culturally different groups would also include cultural validity. Cultural validity is concerned with the procedures necessary to identify the rules that regulate conduct and the rules that define various practices and institutions. Rules of the first kind tell us that certain things ought to be or may be done in a certain manner, whereas rules of the second kind tell us how acts are to be performed. The latter norms provide the system of rules that give structure to such things as marriage, contracts, language, religion, games, play, and so forth. Rules about practices provide the background for conduct.

These rules are at the core of the cultural framework of social groups and knowledge of them is fundamental to understanding culture and cultural differences. Such knowledge, for example, helps the researcher determine if a concept means the same thing to people from different cultures. If it does not, conclusions about differences between cultural groups based on the assumption of shared meaning are invalid (e.g., concluding that individuals in the culture in which the construct is meaningless are deficient). Although the truth or validity of a particular study is impossible to prove, conceptualizations that reflect poor understanding of these rules and subjective meanings clearly is grounds to question the cultural validity of comparative research with culturally different groups (Washington & McLoyd, 1982). The research described in this volume provides examples of some effective ways to discover and operationalize conceptual categories of cultural dimensions for different social groups, ranging from the use of focus groups (see chapters by Cooper; and García Coll & Magnuson), to informal interviewing of individuals during home and neighborhood visits (Durbrow), to participant observations in neighborhood and family activities such as block parties and play activities (Burton & Price-Spratlen).

I believe that increased investment in this step in the research process could result in enormous payoffs in the form of advances in our understanding of cultural processes in children's development. Existing developmental research, in the main, is undergirded by conceptual frameworks developed for thinking about non-Latino White middle-class children, families, and society. The concepts and values at the center of these frameworks often are incompatible with the realities, beliefs, and values of major segments of ethnic and racial minority populations. For example, among Native Americans, tribe or tribal grouping rather than the nuclear family is the important unit of analysis for understanding patterns of organization, family systems, and socialization. Likewise, whereas individual autonomy and competitiveness are strongly held values among White, middle-class individuals, in many minority groups these values are tempered by or rejected in favor of values for interdependence and cooperation (Boykin, 1983; Harrison, Serafica, & McAdoo, 1984; Harrison, Wilson, Pine, Chan, & Buriel, 1990).

Progress in understanding the influence of culture on the development of American children will require formulating and employing more culturally appropriate concepts as well as broadening and reframing theoretical conceptions to reflect the cultural diversity in American society (Dilworth-Anderson, Burton, & Johnson, 1993; Laosa, 1989). Developing and reconfiguring analytic points of departure, too often short-circuited during the course of research investigations, are essential elements in the study of culture and part of the intricate and dynamic processes by which research is made culturally sensitive (Rogler, 1989). This can be an arduous and slow process because of prerequisite empirical and conceptual "spadework." More dynamic than linear in nature, investigatory work of this nature rarely is given high priority by funding agencies because its feasibility and payoffs are seen as more uncertain than is the case for research grounded in traditional, mainstream concepts and frameworks.

Cultural validity also encompasses the question of whether the operationalization of a given psychological construct is valid across different cultural groups, that is, whether assessment tools are accurately measuring the constructs that they are assumed to measure when administered to different social groups. Without the requisite information to make this determination, it is difficult to discern whether group differences or similarities are indications of differences or similarities in psychological processes. Again, researchers interested in cultural influences on development in American children should be prepared to devote considerable resources to addressing the issue of measurement equivalence because, like the conceptual frameworks that determine what is to be measured, extant assessment tools were typically developed in the majority population (i.e., non-Latino White middle-class individuals) and, consequently, may not be measuring the same construct in minority populations. Likewise, because of differences within minority groups (e.g., acculturation status, ethnic identity), it is possible that a measure may not have measurement equivalence across individuals within a single ethnic or racial minority group (Knight & Hill, 1998). Recent years have witnessed major progress in conceptualizing different forms of measurement equivalence (e.g., item, functional, and scalar equivalence) and devising different analytic procedures to verify each type of equivalence (Hui & Triandis, 1985). Suffice it to say verification of measurement equivalence, in the main, involves a determination of the degree to which the reliability and validity coefficients associated with a measure in one group are similar to those in another group (Knight & Hill, 1998).

Interpretative Validity. Cooper and her colleagues attend to another dimension of external validity that should be used to evaluate the adequacy of comparative research with culturally different groups, namely interpretative validity (Washington & McLoyd, 1982). In particular, they held focus groups *following* the collection and analyses of survey data "to link our interpretations with their [the study participants'] experiences" and noted that "these collaborative conversations proved to be key resources, and form the basis for our continuing use of focus groups in our research." The question of whether to utilize the words, motives, interpretations, and explanations as rendered by the informants or to give priority to the interpretations of social scientists is one of the critical methodological questions in comparative research. Fisher and Werner (1978) suggested a credible way out of this dilemma, arguing that anthropologists, and I would add behavioral scientists interested in cultural influences, should begin with "the culturally constituted units, always listening to what people tell us, while looking for the theoretical structure that enables us to understand and interpret what we are hearing, and observing" (p. 215). It is difficult to envision how to judge the interpretative validity of an investigation if research participants or members of their cultural groups have not been given even minimal opportunities to offer their interpretations and explanations of the behavior or phenomenon in question, unfettered by the researcher's perspective.

Conclusion

Marked increases in the proportional representation of ethnic and racial minorities in the American population largely due to immigration obligate the discipline to give increasing priority to understanding cultural processes in children's development. To do otherwise is ethically indefensible and inimical to the long-term self-interests of the nation. Advancements in this area will depend on the extent to which we develop theoretical perspectives that have robust explanatory power, are steeped in basic knowledge about minority cultures, and reflect the integrity of minority cultures. Augmenting the criteria we use to judge the adequacy of comparative research to include cultural and interpretative validity also is likely to enhance the accumulation of knowledge about cultural processes in child development. Meeting the research challenges set forth by the increasing racial, ethnic, and cultural heterogeneity within American society will necessitate proactive responses from all quarters of the discipline, including graduate training programs, funding agencies, professional societies, journal editors, and individual scholars in their roles as researchers, teachers, and reviewers of manuscripts and grant applications.

REFERENCES

Boykin, A. W. (1983). The academic performance of Afro-American children. In J. T. Spence (Ed.), *Achievement and achievement motives* (pp. 324–371). San Francisco: Freeman.

Dilworth-Anderson, P., Burton, L., & Johnson, L. B. (1993). Reframing theories for understanding race, ethnicity, and families. In P. B. Boss, W. Doherty, R. LaRossa, W. R. Schumm, & S. K. Steinmetz (Eds.), *Sourcebook of family theories and methods: A contextual approach* (pp. 627–646). New York: Plenum.

Edelman, M. W. (1987). *Families in peril: An agenda for social change.* Cambridge, MA: Harvard University Press.

Edmondson, B. (1994). The trend you can't ignore. *American Demographics, 16,* 2.

Fisher, L. E., & Werner, O. (1978). Explaining explanation: Tension in American anthropology. *Journal of Anthropological Research, 34,* 194–215.

Guerra, N., & Jagers, R. (1998). The importance of culture in the assessment of children and youth. In V. C. McLoyd & L. Steinberg (Eds.), *Studying minority adolescents: Conceptual, methodological, and theoretical issues* (pp. 167–181). Mahwah, NJ: Lawrence Erlbaum Associates.

Hacker, A. (1992). *Two nations: Black and white, separate, hostile, unequal.* New York: Scribners.

Harrison, A., Serafica, F., & McAdoo, H. (1984). Ethnic families of color. In. R. Parke, R. Emde, H. McAdoo, & G. Sackett (Eds.), *Review of child development research: The family* (Vol. 7, pp. 329–371). Chicago: University of Chicago Press.

Harrison, A., Wilson, M., Pine, C., Chan, S., & Buriel, R. (1990). Family ecologies of ethnic minority children. *Child Development, 61,* 357–362.

House, J. (1981). Social structure and personality. In M. Rosenberg & R. Turner (Eds.), *Social psychology: Sociological perspectives* (pp. 525–561). New York: Basic Books.

Hui, C. H., & Triandis, H. C. (1985). Measurement in cross-cultural psychology: A review and comparison of strategies. *Journal of Cross-Cultural Psychology, 16,* 131–152.

Knight, G. P., & Hill, N. (1998). Measurement equivalence in research involving minority adolescents. In V. C. McLoyd & L. Steinberg (Eds.), *Studying minority adolescents: Conceptual, methodological, and theoretical issues* (pp. 183–210). Mahwah, NJ: Lawrence Erlbaum Associates.

Laosa, L. (1989). Social competence in childhood: Toward a developmental, socioculturally relativistic paradigm. *Journal of Applied Developmental Psychology, 10,* 447–468.

Martin, P. L. (1994). Good intentions gone awry: IRCA and U.S. agriculture. *Annals of the American Academy of Political and Social Science, 534,* 44–57.

Martin, P., & Midgley, E. (1994). Immigration to the United States: Journey to an uncertain destination. *Population Bulletin, 49*(2), 2–45.

McLoyd, V. C. (1998). Changing demographics in the American population: Implications for research on minority children and adolescents. In V. C. McLoyd & L. Steinberg (Eds.), *Studying minority adolescents: Conceptual, methodological, and theoretical issues* (pp. 3–28). Mahwah, NJ: Lawrence Erlbaum Associates.

Portes, A., & Zhou, M. (1993). The new second generation: Segmented assimilation and its variants. *Annals of the American Academy of Political and Social Sciences, 530,* 74–96.

Portes, A., & Zhou, M. (1994). Should immigrants assimilate? *Public Interest, 116*, 18–33.

Rogler, L. (1989). The meaning of culturally sensitive research in mental health. *American Journal of Psychiatry, 146*, 296–303.

Sontag, D. (1993, June 29). A fervent "no" to assimilation in new America: Children of immigrants rewriting an axiom. *The New York Times*, p. A6.

U.S. Bureau of the Census (1994). *Statistical abstract of the United States: 1994.* Washington, DC: US Government Printing Office.

Washington, E. D., & McLoyd, V. C. (1982). The external validity of research involving American minorities. *Human Development, 25*, 324–339.

Weisner, T. S., Gallimore, R., & Jordan, C. (1988). Unpackaging cultural effects on classroom learning: Native Hawaiian peer assistance and child-generated activity. *Anthropology and Education Quarterly, 19*, 327–351.

Wetzel, J. (1987). *American youth: A statistical snapshot.* New York: William T. Grant Foundation.

Yemma, J. (1997, December 28). "Whiteness Studies" targets racial healing. *The Herald-Sun*, Durham, NC, pp. G3, G8.

Chapter 7

Culture and Development in Our Poststructural Age

Richard A. Shweder
University of Chicago

This year's Minnesota Symposium, which takes place in the thick of the revival of "cultural psychology" as a discipline (see e.g., Bruner, 1990; Cole, 1996; D'Andrade, 1995; Goodnow, Miller, & Kessel, 1995; Greenfield, 1997; Jessor, Colby, & Shweder, 1996; Markus, Kitayama, & Heiman, 1997; Miller, 1997; Much, 1992; Rogoff, 1990; Shore, 1996; Shweder, 1991, 1993; Shweder & Sullivan, 1993; Shweder, Goodnow, Hatano, LeVine, Markus, & Miller, 1997; Stigler, Shweder, & Herdt, 1991; Wierzbicka, 1991, 1992), is about "Cultural Processes of Child Development." My aim in this chapter is to locate this year's symposium in an historical context by telling a story about some of the major changes that have taken place over the past 30 years in our picture of mental development. I take account of the current interest in cultural processes of child development by drawing a contrast between the once fashionable structural (primarily Piagetian) picture of mental development (which left rather little intellectual space for the study of cultural psychology) and various pictures of mental development from out of our current poststructural age (which make room for almost everything, including culture).

PIAGET'S GRAND STRUCTURAL PICTURE OF MENTAL DEVELOPMENT

In 1966, when I entered graduate school in the Department of Social Relations at Harvard University, the mind and spirit of Jean Piaget was a vibrant presence in William James Hall and his "structural" stage theory

137

of cognitive development was the rage in most leading centers of developmental psychology in the United States (see Piaget, 1954, 1967, 1970). Here is the version of Piaget's theory that was current and quickly passed on to students in those days.

For one thing it was emphasized that Piaget studied *cognitive* development. Although the relevant contrast set was often left a bit vague (cognition versus what? Behavior? Conation? Emotion? Nonrepresentational thought?) it was made relatively clear to us by our teachers that the fact that Piaget studied *cognitive* development meant at least these two things: (a) that he studied the mind of the child the way one might study the mind of an ideal scientist or a logician, and (b) that from a Piagetian perspective growth or development had something to do with endorsing true propositions.

The study of cognitive development was thereby differentiated from the study of development in noncognitive domains, such as emotional development or the development of moral character. In those noncognitive domains, we were told, development did not amount to endorsing true propositions but rather amounted instead to actually doing what is right or good (as in the case of having moral character) or amounted to actually experiencing appropriate feelings and desires in various kinds of social situations (as in the case of being emotionally competent or mature). Feeling, desire, and moral commitment were thus placed outside the territory of the cognitive domain, whereas scientific, logical, and propositional reasoning were placed securely within the field of cognitive studies.

We learned that Piaget studied the development of scientific and logical capacities in the child by carefully observing children striving to figure out what causes what, striving for consistency among ideas, striving to build up or construct for themselves a set of principles (e.g., the logic of inductive science and experimental reasoning, the idea of necessary truths) for regulating their own thought and for avoiding intellectual mistakes. Heroic images were presented to us of Piaget on a kind of researcher's Odyssey to the most unlikely of places in his quest for a grand all-encompassing theory of mental development—images of Piaget playing marbles with children in the playground, of Piaget as the assiduous chronicler of the sucking behavior of infants in the nursery.

We were told that Piaget had traced the ontogenetic history of children's scientific and logical understandings through four self-constructed stages: the sensorimotor, preoperational, concrete operational, and formal operational stages. At each stage new mental structures were said to emerge: the idea of an object during the sensorimotor stage, the idea of reversibility and transitivity during the concrete operational stage. Thus, for example, a preoperational 4-year-old was supposed to lack the requisite mental structures for constructing the perspective of others as evidenced by the following type of interview (reported by Peter Wason) with a 4-year-old: "Do you have a brother?" "Yes." "What's his name?" "Jim." "Does Jim have a brother?" "No."

In 1966, when I entered graduate school, psychology in America had long since lost its institutional connection to philosophy. Perhaps that is why no one bothered to point out to us that the core ideas examined by Piaget (number, object, cause, space, time, morality) were more or less the same ideas identified by Immanuel Kant as synthetic *a priori* truths and as the necessary preconditions of empiricism, for without some *a priori* idea of number, object, cause, space, and time the very notion of "having an experience" (the supposed source of all knowledge for empiricists) makes no sense. Perhaps that is why no one bothered to boggle our minds and disrupt the Piagetian developmental story by asking "how is it possible for a young infant to experience anything at all (including your experimental manipulation) if he or she does not already have at hand (or in its mouth) the ideas that Piaget says are not available until 18 months, or 6-years-of-age, or what have you?"

What we did learn was that according to Piagetian theory immature thinking (in contrast to mature thinking) was characterized by a cluster of correlated attributes. Immature thinking was supposed to be undifferentiated (vs. differentiated), concrete (vs. abstract), egocentric or subject-dependent (vs. impersonal or objective), context-bound (vs. context-free), inconsistent (vs. consistent), incomplete (vs. complete), intuitive (vs. reflective), implicit (vs. explicit), complexive, associative, or functional (vs. taxonomic), percept-driven (vs. concept-driven), animistic (vs. causal), temporal (vs. logical), affective in tone and concrete in its imagery. Young children were said to be unaware of any perspective but their own. They were said to be unable to distinguish a word or name from its referent, unable to know the difference between objectivity and subjectivity.

Moreover a kind of master developmental narrative got built up, in which the French Enlightenment's opposition between religion–superstition–irrationality versus logic–science–rationality was used to tell a story, indeed the very same story, about the difference between children versus adults, about the difference between primitive peoples versus civilized peoples, and about the difference between premodern peoples in the West (e.g., people in the dark ages) and modern peoples in the West (peoples who benefited from the French Enlightenment).

The basic theme of the narrative, which was sometimes explicit and sometimes covert, went like this: In contrast to mature thinkers or the enlightened elite (we presumed that meant us), all those "others" (children, contemporary primitive peoples, and historical peoples from the premodern period in the West) are relatively confused or undifferentiated about a lot of things. They are confused about the relationship of language to reality (for example, they believe in "word magic" or the idea that symbols are part of the reality they describe). They are confused about the relationship of the moral order to the natural world (e.g., they believe in "immanent justice" or the idea that suffering is punishment for your sins). They are confused about the relationship of the social order to the natural world (e.g., they tend to think that their duties, obligations, and social roles are objective emanations or have been handed down by God). And so forth.

PICTURES OF MENTAL DEVELOPMENT FROM OUT
OF OUR POSTSTRUCTURAL AGE

Before going any further in the telling of this tale I want to confess that I am of the opinion that any American psychologist who is unfeigned in his or her assessment of the recent history of child development studies must admit that interest in that Piagetian picture of mental development had largely waned by the early 1980s and that today, at least in the United States among developmental psychologists, Piaget's research agenda is now more or less moribund. It is not even clear that his spirit lives on, although knowledge of some standardized and watered down version of his stage theory may still be required to pass a licensing exam in child psychiatry in some states or an introductory psychology test at some university.

Today, rightly or wrongly, at most leading centers of cognitive developmental psychology in the United States, students are told a different story. The story they are told is out of a poststructural age. Perhaps it is the master narrative of an age that is suspicious of all master narratives and totalizing world views and does not worry quite so much as did Piaget about the role of self-monitoring, rational justification, and contradiction in fostering conceptual (and behavioral) change. Piaget was a modernist and we live in a postmodern age.

The current poststructural story has many themes and no one has integrated them into a single plot (which may be part of the point of the story) but some of the themes go something like this:

1. The mind is not a structured whole. If we examine the actual cognitive functioning of individuals across a series of tasks we discover that no single operational level is a generalized property of an individual's thought. Thus, as the poststructural story goes, Piaget exaggerated the stage-like character of cognitive growth.

2. The mind should not be conceptualized as a central processing unit organized by means of abstract operational structures. The mind is decentralized, modular and concrete. What you think about is decisive for how

you think. Thus, as the poststructural story goes, Piaget misjudged the role of "mere content" and domain-specific knowledge in reasoning, judgment, and memory.

3. The mind of the child is differentiated and complex from the start. Kant's synthetic *a priori* truths (object permanence, number, time, space, causality) are hard-wired as innate ideas. The newly born already know a lot from the deep past. Thus, as the story goes (and here arguably the story is more premodern than poststructural and how the various themes fit together remains to be seen) Piaget underestimated the intellectual sophistication and operational capacity of infants and young children. We come into the world old not young.

4. There is no property of thought that can serve as a general index of intellectual immaturity. The various properties of thinking (concrete vs. abstract, intuitive vs. reflective, functional vs. taxonomic, context-bound vs. context-free, temporal vs. logical, emotion-laden vs. affect-free, etc.) that were supposed to serve of indicators of mental development do not necessarily correlate with each other, and out of context they are not reliable measures of mental immaturity. There are advanced modes of thought where performers are expert and sophisticated precisely because they are concrete, percept-driven, imagistic, context-bound, emotion-laden, and so on. Thus, as the poststructural story goes, Piaget mythologized and totalized the unidirectional nature of progressive conceptual change.

According to the story told these days it is an entirely open question whether the newly born come into the world with an overabundance of specific and contradictory propensities, some of which are selected for and others suppressed by cultural practices in the course of development (the "maintenance-loss" approach to socialization; Werker, 1989), whether the newly born come into the world (as Piaget believed) with only a few specific propensities (e.g., a sucking reflex) which are then elaborated and gener- alized in the course of development, or whether the newly born come into the world with either a lot or a few highly general propensities (e.g., to "categorize"—treat like cases alike and different cases differently) that are then specified and given character in the course of development.

I have contributed to this story. I like this story. I even believe in this story. There are themes in this story that I have narrated before in other publications. Nevertheless there is, I believe, at least one motif that has yet to receive sufficient attention in the poststructural literature: the tension between rationalism and pluralism in Piaget's account of mental develop- ment. In the remainder of this chapter I suggest that any credible post- structural theory of mental development must find a way to marry ration- alism and cultural pluralism, which is a match that Piaget was disinclined to make.

IS IT POSSIBLE TO BE A DEVELOPMENTALIST
AND A CULTURAL PLURALIST AT THE SAME TIME?

In my view any credible poststructural story about mental development must engage and come to terms with Piaget's rationalistic conception of the process of mental development. As a rationalist who studied conceptual change Piaget believed that what *deserved* to be called mature thinking (or correct mental functioning) could be characterized in terms of strictly objective ideals or standards (e.g., the rules of logic, the abstract principle of justice). Piaget thus believed that what *deserved* to be called mature thinking was the same across cultures and history. He believed that when people disagree about what is true there are principles, methods, or procedures that can reconcile their differences and produce agreement. Most developmentalists who take *culture* at all seriously have some difficulties with this aspect of Piaget's rationalism. So I am going to try to soften the idea of objective standards and rational justifiability. I am going to do this to make room for the relevance of a developmental perspective to cases where the standards and ideals that guide development and define mature thinking are contingent, contestable, plural, culture-specific and thus not universally binding.

The remainder of this chapter is thus about Piaget's rationalistic conception of the process of mental development, which I believe is separable from his monistic view of the mature product of that process. Piaget believed that the route to mature thinking (mental development) was (a) a temporal process (it took time to become a mature thinker); (b) a progressive process (over time more mature understandings superseded less mature understandings); and (c) an active process (over time more mature understandings superseded less mature understandings because individuals are self-reflective knowers who try to work out and see for themselves the rational justification for their own understandings). In praise of this aspect of Piaget's theory I argue that his very Hegelian conception of the process of mental development is entirely right-minded and is so alien to the philosophical assumptions of both empirical psychology and poststructural thinking in the United States that it has largely been overlooked or misunderstood.

Before I offer some tokens of respect for aspects of Piaget's rationalism, however, I have two other confessions to make. My first confession is that I am an anthropologist. More specifically I am an anthropological pluralist interested in different modes of thought and understanding among adults in different cultural traditions around the world. Over the years I have given special attention to Brahmanical Hindu traditions in India and secular liberal humanist traditions in the United States.

Anthropological pluralists are distrustful of certain applications of the Piagetian principle that what *deserves* to be called mature thinking (or correct mental functioning) is the same across cultures and history. They become especially suspicious when a developmental theory is proposed by the lights of which the thinking (or mental functioning) of full grown adults in other cultures begins to look very much like the thinking of young children in our own.

For example, in his account of the Swiss child's idea of "immanent justice" Piaget makes it quite clear that he believes that there is a *universally binding* rational standard or ideal which defines mature thinking in this domain. In particular this rational standard or ideal is attained by endorsing the proposition that "wickedness may go unpunished and virtue remain unrewarded." Because the belief in immanent justice consists of endorsing the alternative proposition that "justice is a law of nature according to which for every transgression there is some natural catastrophe that serves as its punishment" the endorsement of immanent justice is viewed as an immature or less developed mode of thought. Yet as every anthropologist knows, something very much like a belief in immanent justice can be found not only in the thinking of Swiss 5- and 6-year-olds. It can also be found in the thinking of many millions of South Asian Hindu adults who believe in the idea of "karma" and among adults in many other cultures of the world. Are we to say that the beliefs of Hindu adults are immature or child-like? Are we to draw the opposite and equally invidious conclusion that Northern European children begin life as sophisticated Hindus and then fall into immaturity or regress as they age?

Anthropological pluralists are deeply suspicious of this kind of application of developmental theory, in which by means of some presumptively universalized standard for rational or mature thinking, adults in other cultures are analogized to children in our own, with the implication that they are intellectually immature. Margaret Mead (1932) long ago argued this point with Piaget over the issue of animistic thinking. She argued that among the Manus people of New Guinea it is the adults not the children who are the animists. She suggested that if one adopts the cultural perspective of Manus adults it is European adults who will appear to be intellectually immature because they think like Manus children. She preferred to view both Swiss adults and Manus adults as intellectually mature, each in their own way. Her view was that certain kinds of applications of developmental standards (presumptively universalizing the standard) smack of ethnocentrism and give developmental theory a bad name.

It seems to me that one very obvious implication of Mead's critique is that there are certain kinds of culture-specific standards or ideals for development that should not be applied or generalized to other populations. But it also seems to me that a second and less noted implication of her pluralistic view is that within a particular interpretive community or cultural context those very same ideals can serve perfectly well as developmental standards for children and adults trying to work through for themselves (self-construct) the rational basis of their own traditions. Presumably it would be a matter of some concern among the Manus if their children never intellectually matured and constructed for themselves a defensible and locally rational animistic interpretation of the causal forces of nature.

This discomfort among anthropological pluralists with certain types of applications of developmental theory arises with respect to many other areas of knowledge. For example, adult thinking in much of Hindu society about the status and meaning of dreams (they are not thought to be merely subjective), about the power of words to influence biological and physical nature (mantras, kirtans and other verbal formulas are thought to be effective), and about the moral basis of hierarchy (*autonomy* is not privileged over *heteronomy*) is reminiscent of early Piagetian accounts of the ideas and understandings of Western children. Indeed, I suspect that one reason Piaget himself moved from those earlier accounts (which were focused on children's understandings of dreams, words, and punishment) to the later stages of his research (where he focused on children's understanding of number, chance, and logical necessity) was to accommodate criticism. In the process of constructing his own theory of the world he found a way to hold on to the view that what deserves to be called mature thinking can be characterized in terms of strictly objective ideals and standards and is the same across cultures and history. His way of doing this was to radically narrow the types of domains of knowledge (experimental reasoning—yes, dream understandings—no) to which his type of developmental analysis should be applied. In effect he adopted the premise common to all "structural" approaches: viz., the premise that human beings would all think the same way (reason the same way, make the same judgments) if it weren't for differences in the content of their thought. Looking back on his own early research informed by his subsequently constructed structural theory, I suspect Piaget must have viewed those early investigations of children's ideas about dreams, word meanings, and immanent justice as somewhat misguided studies of mere content. Mere content, he might have reasoned, is not proper grist for developmental structural analysis.

PIAGET'S CHALLENGE TO ANTHROPOLOGY

The second confession I want to make is that I have been a critic of Piaget (e.g., Shweder, 1982, 1984). I have gone so far as to suggest that research on mental development in children can be advanced by inverting his assumptions ("standing Piaget on his head") and by paying far more attention than did Piaget to assisted learning, to the discretionary or extralogical aspects of mental development, to the way content is part of the process of thought and thus what you think about is decisive for how you think, and to the socialization of cultural ideals for development.

Nevertheless there are two appealing features of Piaget's conception of mental development to which I want to draw attention. Piaget believed that "logic is the morality of thought just as morality is the logic of action." Although this may be too narrow a view of the "morality of thought," Piaget's formulation makes it clear that (a) in his view the study of mental development is primarily a prescriptive rather than a merely descriptive discipline; (b) that having good reasons and justifications for what you think and do is a driving engine of conceptual change; and (c) that *logic* is not just another domain of knowledge or specialized module of mind.

I will not discuss "c" in this context, except to note that it is quite fashionable these days, in our poststructural age, to argue that logic is just one more specialized module of thought or domain of knowledge like recognizing faces or speaking a natural language. The alternative view is that logic is an essential even if incomplete part of the rationality internal to any domain of knowledge. This view has credibility in my mind because it is hard to understand how the *justification* of reasoning and decision making in any domain of knowledge could proceed without the presence within that domain and every domain of something like a logic device.

Piaget's commitment to the study of mental development as a prescriptive science and to the process of self-justification as an engine of conceptual change are the features of his thinking that I believe are most worthy of praise. He recognized that the idea of human development implies much more than change over time, that it implies some desirable state of mental functioning the ultimate attainment of which is a mark of progress.

These aspects of Piaget's thinking are especially challenging for my own discipline of anthropology, which is well known for its emphasis on the existence of plurality or diversity in the descriptive norms of cultures around the world. Thus for example, anthropologists will tell you that it is *normal* (in the descriptive sense) for Samburu girls in Kenya to be circumcised during adolescence, that it is *normal* (in the descriptive sense) in India for widows not to be invited to a wedding ceremony because their presence is normally thought to be inauspicious, that it is *normal* (in the descriptive sense) for American midlife adults to put their own parents out to pasture in an old age home rather than care for them in their own household. Speaking as an anthropologist, if I were to describe for you *normal* medical cognition in rural India, I would start by pointing out that given the normal metaphysical belief system subscribed to by hundreds of millions of Hindus, when physical or mental suffering occurs the diagnostic situation is, from the native point of view, understandably quite complex. For one thing, there is not just one world to deal with but three: the society of the gods (who are a major presence in nearly every household and

community), the society of the spirits, including the spirits of dead ancestors (who are also a major presence in almost every household and community), and the society of human beings. Moreover it is normally believed
that these three worlds all interact in a universe governed by the principles
of "dharma" (objective obligations emanating from God) and the laws of
"karma" (the idea that nature guarantees that in the long run for every
action there is a just and proportionate reaction).

Notice however that these anthropological claims about the existence
of plurality or diversity in the norms of different cultures amount to little
more than the proposition that there is variety in what people around the
world believe and desire. They do not come close to touching on the far
more challenging issues raised by Piaget rationalism: Is there variety in
what is believable not just in what is believed? Is there plurality in what is
desirable not just in what is desired? Is it really possible for mental states
that are pathological, irrational, or immature in one community to be
healthy, rational, and mature in another?

Piaget's strict notions of objectivity and rational justifiability blocked
him from seeing how the answer to these questions might be "yes." Ironically most poststructural pluralistic anthropologists who might intuitively
believe that the answer to those questions is *yes* have yet to realize that
issues of justification are at the heart of cultural analysis. They have yet to
realize that the mere existence of variety in cultural beliefs and desires
does not imply that it is possible to be mentally developed and intellectually
mature in culturally divergent ways.

Piaget's challenge to anthropology is to demonstrate how particular
cultural understandings and practices can seem well-founded and compel-
ling precisely because they have been developmentally constructed out of
the self-reflective processes of rational individuals. His challenge to anthropology is to show how autonomous reason depends upon cultural tradition
to exercise its critical powers. His challenge to anthropology is to formulate
an ideal of rationality (and an account of the role of metaphysical beliefs in
the construction of our sense of reality) that will make it credible to be a
developmentalist and a pluralist at the very same time. When that challenge
has been substantially met, cultural psychology will have come of age.

Author's Note

This commentary draws on and develops certain ideas about our poststructural age that were presented at the Conference on "The Growing Mind,"
Centennial Celebration of Jean Piaget's Birth, Geneva, Switzerland, Sep-
tember 14–18, 1996, in an unpublished paper entitled "Piaget's Challenge
to Anthropology: Stories and Remarks From the Post-Structural Age." The
paper was delivered in Geneva at the Invited Symposium on "Cognitive

Development Beyond Childhood: Wisdom and the Pragmatics of Life," chaired by Paul Baltes.

ACKNOWLEDGMENT

In preparing this essay I am grateful to the MacArthur Foundation Research Network on Successful Midlife Development (MIDMAC) for its generous support.

REFERENCES

Bruner, J. S. (1990). *Acts of meaning.* Cambridge, MA: Harvard University Press.

Cole, M. (1996). *Cultural psychology: A once and future discipline.* Cambridge, MA: Harvard University Press.

D'Andrade, R. (1995). *The development of cognitive anthropology.* New York: Cambridge University Press.

Goodnow, J., Miller, P., & Kessel, F. (Eds.). (1995). *New directions for child development: Vol. 67. Cultural practices as contexts for development.* San Francisco: Jossey-Bass.

Greenfield, P. (1997). Culture as process: Empirical methodology for cultural psychology. In J. W. Berry, Y. H. Poortinga, & J. Pandey (Eds.), *Handbook of cross-cultural psychology: Vol. 1. Theory and method.* Boston: Allyn & Bacon.

Jessor, R., Colby, A., & Shweder, R. A. (1996). *Ethnography and human development: Context and meaning in social inquiry.* Chicago: University of Chicago Press.

Markus, H., Kitayama, S., & Heiman, R. J. (1997). Culture and "basic" psychological principles. In E. T. Higgins & A. W. Kruglanski (Eds.), *Social psychology: Handbook of basic principles.* New York: Guilford.

Mead, M. (1932). An investigation of the thought of primitive children, with special reference to animism. *Journal of the Royal Anthropological Institute, 62,* 173–190.

Miller, J. G. (1997). Theoretical issues in cultural psychology and social constructionism. In J. W. Berry, Y. Poortinga, & J. Pandey (Eds.), *Handbook of cross-cultural psychology: Vol. 1. Theory and method.* Boston: Allyn & Bacon.

Much, N. C. (1992). The analysis of discourse as methodology for a semiotic psychology. *American Behavioral Scientist, 36,* 52–72.

Piaget, J. (1954). *The construction of reality in the child.* New York: Basic Books.

Piaget, J. (1967). *Six psychological studies.* New York: Random House.

Piaget, J. (1970). *Structuralism.* New York: Basic Books.

Rogoff, B. (1990). *Apprenticeship in thinking: Cognitive development in social context.* New York: Oxford University Press.

Shore, B. (1996). *Culture in mind: Culture, cognition and the problem of meaning.* New York: Oxford University Press.

Shweder, R. A. (1982). On savages and other children. *American Anthropologist, 84,* 354–366.

Shweder, R. A. (1984). Anthropology's romantic rebellion against the enlightenment: Or, there is more to thinking than reason and evidence. In R. A. Shweder & R. A. LeVine (Eds.), *Culture theory: Essays on mind, self and emotion.* New York: Cambridge University Press.

Shweder, R. A. (1991). *Thinking through cultures: Expeditions in cultural psychology.* Cambridge, MA: Harvard University Press.

Shweder, R. A. (1993). The cultural psychology of the emotions. In M. Lewis & J. Haviland (Eds.), *Handbook of emotions*. New York: Guilford.

Shweder, R. A., & Sullivan, M. (1993). Cultural psychology: Who needs it? *Annual Review of Psychology, 44*, 497–523.

Shweder, R. A., Goodnow, J., Hatano, G., LeVine, R., Markus, H., & Miller, P. (1997). The cultural psychology of development: One mind, many mentalities. In W. Damon (Ed.), *Handbook of child psychology: Vol. 1. Theoretical models of human development*. New York: Wiley.

Stigler, J., Shweder, R. A., & Herdt, G. (Eds.). (1990). *Cultural psychology: Essays on comparative human development*. New York: Cambridge University Press.

Werker, J. (1989). Becoming a native listener. *American Scientist, 77*, 54–59.

Wierzbicka, A. (1991). *Cross-cultural pragmatics: The semantics of human interaction*. New York: Mouton de Gruyer.

Wierzbicka, A. (1992). *Semantics, culture and cognition: Universal human concepts in culture-specific configurations*. New York: Oxford University Press.

Author Index

Subject Index